Mongolian Études

Mongolian Études

TO THE ENDS OF AN EMPIRE
A REMARKABLE STORY TOLD IN LETTERS, POEMS AND PROSE

Vladimir Azarov

EXILE
editions
Fiction, Poetry, Translation, Drama and Exhibition

Library and Archives Canada Cataloguing in Publication

Azarov, Vladimir, 1935-, author
    Mongolian études : to the ends of an empire : a remarkable story told in letters, poems and prose / Vladimir Azarov.

Poems.
ISBN 978-1-55096-356-4 (pbk.)

    I. Title.

PS8601.Z37M66 2013   C811'.6   C2013-903997-X

Design and Composition by Michael Callaghan
Typeset in Calisto, Times New Roman, Fairfield, Bodoni, Minion, Carlton, Trajan and Poetica Chanceryl fonts at the Moons of Jupiter Studios

Published by Exile Editions Ltd ~ www.ExileEditions.com
144483 Southgate Road 14 – GD, Holstein, Ontario, N0G 2A0
Printed and Bound in Canada in 2013, by Imprimerie Gauvin

We gratefully acknowledge the Canada Council for the Arts, the Government of Canada through the Canada Book Fund (CBF), the Ontario Arts Council, and the Ontario Media Development Corporation, for their support toward our publishing activities.

Canadian Sales: The Canadian Manda Group, 165 Dufferin Street,
Toronto ON M6K 3H6   www.mandagroup.com   416 516 0911

North American and International Distribution, and U.S. Sales:
Independent Publishers Group, 814 North Franklin Street,
Chicago IL 60610   www.ipgbook.com   toll free: 1 800 888 4741

for Namsraijav Ochir

One arrow alone can be easily broken,
but many arrows are indestructible.

—GENGHIS KHAN

PROLOGUE

Toronto, Canada
October 12, 2012

Extraordinary and Plenipotentiary Ambassador
of the Russian Federation in Mongolia
Samoilenko Viktor Vasilievich

Dear Viktor Vasilievich,

I am an architect. I grew up in Kazakhstan, and studied in
Moscow. In the early 1970s, I supervised the building of the
Russian Embassy in Mongolia. I now live in Canada, where I've
become a writer-poet. Presently, I am writing about the years
surrounding the building of that embassy in Ulan-Bator decades
ago. I recall an outstanding Mongolian woman who worked as a
supervisor for the Mongolian government. She became my friend.
She had studied at Leningrad University and had been a friend of
the remarkable ethnologist, Lev Gumilev; she had also been
acquainted with Lev Gumilev's mother—the great Russian poet,
Anna Akhmatova.

Decades have passed since I was in Mongolia and time has blotted the name of the woman. I would really like to dedicate my
book to her. Dear Viktor Vasilievich, I apologize for this request,
but I am asking you to help me to find, in the embassy archives,
the name of this woman.

I appreciate your help and I am sorry for the time this will take, not just by yourself but by the busy workers who will have to be involved in such a search.

Sincerely,
Vladimir Azarov

Embassy of Russian Federation in Mongolia
N 624
November 19, 2012
To V.P. Azarov

Dear Vladimir Pavlovich,

In response to your request that we help you to find the name of
the Mongolian woman who curated the construction of our
embassy building in Ulan-Bator on behalf of the embassy itself,
and who was also a friend of Lev Gumilev, we are pleased to
inform you that:

It is the opinion of several veterans at the Mongolian Ministry of
Foreign Affairs that she is most probably one Namsraijav Ochir
(among Mongols, she was known familiarly as Ina Ochir).

Colleagues helped connect us to her daughter, Gerel, who is a
professor at the Mongolian State University. She has confirmed
that her mother was a friend of L.N. Gumilev while she was a
student at Leningrad State University. Gerel also has in her
possession correspondence between her mother and the famous
scientist. Gerel is prepared to answer your questions.

Yours Sincerely,
Ambassador Viktor Vasilievich Samoilenko

Toronto, Canada
November 21, 2012

Dear Gerel,

I am the one who is hunting for information about your mother.
I am writing a book about my business trip to Ulan-Bator when I
was the architect supervising the Russian Embassy construction
project in Mongolia. Your mother acted as supervisor of
construction on behalf of the Mongolian government. Your
mother Namsraijav Ochir is central to my tale, a book of poetry
that is almost finished. I'd like to know some details of your
mother's life. I have several questions. If you can help me, I
would deeply appreciate it. So will my readers.

As I remember, she was an outstanding woman, highly educated,
loved art, and was a friend of Lev Gumilev. Dear Gerel, it would
make me very happy if you were to share private information
with me for my book.

All the best!
Sincerely,
Vladimir Azarov

Ulan-Bator, Mongolia
November 23, 2012

Dear Vladimir Pavlovich,

I was glad to get your letter. It is very pleasing to me that you are writing about Mongolia and my mother. I saw your website. I am glad that you have adapted so successfully to Canada. I have visited Canada many times, having taken part in a joint project with Saint Mary's University in Halifax. Also, I have participated in several scientific symposiums in Quebec City and Toronto. I have many friends and colleagues in Canada.

I shall try to answer your questions. My mother was not an ordinary person, she was highly educated, an interesting conversationalist, steeped in music, painting, astronomy, botany and many other fields, such as the history of religion.

I once wanted to write a book about my memories of her, that was in a distant time. My mother died eight years ago, and I am now busy with my students, projects, and work in several international organizations. Your letter reminds me that I'd wanted to write a tribute to my mother.

Best wishes,
Gerel

Toronto, Canada
Monday, November 26, 2012

Dear Gerel,

Your material is amazing! Your memories of your mother, of
the brutal Stalin years, remain topical. I have let my publisher
know about what you've sent me. Familiar with Russian history,
he is happy to publish your material as an appendix to my book.

Your mother's life began in tragedy. I really like her writing,
her style, it is very free, conversational, alive and natural. I am
having it translated. I will keep you informed.

Thank you very much.

Vladimir

THE TIES THAT BIND

Head-in-my-hands
On my first Mongolian
Night I was holed up in a hotel
Where two Finnish men
From the elevator company Kone, had,
The day before,
Booked me into their room,
Leaving behind
A single menacing
Neck-tie
Hanging there in the sky of an
Empty closet—

THE ENDLESS MONOTONY

The endless monotony of the view
Through the wide windows of the car

The gap between Darkhan & Ulan-Bator
A hollow space, scarred orange,

A sighting from Mars
Intimations of rarefied air

An empty backlit
Scrim of sky

Behind Euclidian
Hills upon hills upon hills

Of bald grasslands
That reach out beyond the horizon

Into a monstrous darkness
A thrumming pressure in my ears

Stasis, the deafening silence
Of Mongolia—planet unto itself

Of pummelled space
Hands held high free as the

Flinty-eyed birds who hang in mid-air
Tracking the itinerant

Inhabitants of the steppe
Saiga herds

A large lonely horse & a camel
Flocks of sheep & moles

Gnawing, scampering from hole to hole
No sign of human life—

A relentless erosion
Of slopes emerged from

Mountains beveled by ice
Millions of years ago, no roads, none

Our caravan
Of two cars is stalled!

We're stunned—
My two attendant men sit in silence,

Hands open in supplication,
Knees locked, wearing calf-high boots,

My two camel drivers turned
Chauffeurs, who kiss

Their blind & broken metal beasts
Seeking intervention,

While I, like an ancient Scythian, sit brooding
Under a dark red hanging sky

I

NAMSRAIJAV

BROKEN GLASS

An old set of crystal wine glasses
But—oh!
One of them got broken
On the night before
Christmas:
Miserable in
My loneliness—
I thought, sparkling
Cava Codorniu—a litre of
Wine from Spain, and a soft-spoken woman
Might ameliorate
My melancholy—and
So: as I drank the whole bottle
She drank to me
Only with her eyes

After loading our glasses into
The dishwasher—and before falling asleep—
I heard
Pinging—ping ping ping
One of my long-stemmed crystals,
Wrongly stacked
In the rack, broken

My splendid six, a set!
The loss of this
Wine glass
Marks the beginning
Of the story!
(And the beginning of
A sad *pinging*
In my ears!)

I'd come to Ulan-Bator
To oversee
The Construction of the Soviet
Embassy—
I was a young
Provincial
Among provincials,
A little stern,
A Nose-to-the-Grindstone
Kind of guy,
A Soviet Architect
Carrying official
Blueprints and Drawings
Under my arm,
Ready to render
The finishing touches to

All the rooms,
Even the choosing of tiles, textiles, and
Antiques
For the interiors—

Welcomed in January,
Bussed on the cheek
By the Ambassador's wife!
The First Lady
Of the Russian Embassy, Mongolia!
By June
The six crystal wine
Glasses had been given to me
Along with a
Soviet-Mongolian
Certificate of Merit,
The profile of Lenin embossed in
Raspberry Red!

(Oh, the recent sad sound of
Broken glass!)
By the end of December, I'd prepared a table
For a New Year's Eve party
With several open-hearted contractors of Construction

Who spoke a forceful Russian,
Erupting into
Bellicose laughter

Crystal glasses
Cradled in the calloused
Hands of working men,
Glasses filled to the brim with
Arkhi—a Russian vodka
Straight from the still!
By three in the morning
I could hear bottles
Rolling on the floor,
The *clank clink clank* of dead soldiers
Under the table!
I closed my eyes
And did not
Open them
Until late morning…

That was back when
There was a so-called
International Style of architecture!
(Mies van der Rohe's Seagram building
In New York had been

Established as the standard in
The influential journal—*L'Architecture
d'Aujourd'hui*—our architectural French
Bible!)—
No indulgence in decorative
Details!—a lean yet yielding
Geometric line—

Mies seemed so easy
To imitate (to those of us
Who were foolish): his
Determined
Puritanical clarity,
A post-war clearing away of all the rubble to
Arrive at the rescue of minimalism,
Clarity as a gesture to itself!
Embracing what
We called the GOLDEN MEAN or GOLDEN RATIO—
In accordance with the Greek
Idea of Just
Proportion, Balance—

Le Corbusier had
Brought exactly this self-
Conscious awareness of the Mean back

To architectural design—
A wall, a window, door, ceiling, etc.—you set out
To find an ideal dimensional relationship
Within the working volume!
Where you had a
Façade, for example,
You needed to account for the correlation between
What was horizontal and what was
Vertical within the Whole—

Let "A" and "B" be two
Figures—proportionality would then result in a
Processed ideal, just as a
Division of "A" by "B"
Gives us the Greek "phi °"
—1,6180339887...—
No matter how many
Drafts, sketches, drawings, proposals!
It is always the same—phi °!
—1,6180339887...—
A serious playing (as the French
Think of play being serious) with
Proportion!

"Glass? Metal? Here!
Oh my dear Vladimir Pavlovich,
Comrade Architect!"
(This, from
An aging architect
Who knew something about International Style—
I'd let him see the
Proposals I had placed before
The Soviet Authorities—
So many
Drafts, so many Authorities…)

"Here—in Mongolia—here,
Can you imagine—
Storms, the punishing
Wind in the summer?—and,
The driven winter snow?
Imagine a
Glass box with a cladding of
Polished American whisper-thin metal!
Ha!—a ballerina *en pointe*
In a Mongolian potato field!"

This was back in the hangover days
Of leftover dialectical materialism

And Stalinist Gothic,
The years of The Thaw—
Between Khrushchev and
Brezhnev—years of utter stagnation
When Muscovites
HAD FORGOTTEN how to remember the Mean,
And were unable to openly embrace
The avant-garde in architecture!
Own! Russian!
Constructivism!

Strolling
Through the hills behind the
Embassy construction site,
I hoped to meet
An ancient Hun—a wild nomadic man
On his camel—
(I'd read
About the Huns
In the Lenin Library near the Kremlin—
Together with the
Russian researchers of Mongolia—
Przhevalsky, Kozlov and Pozdneev—
I dived into the history
Of the Mongolian Plateau with the Gobi Desert
n the middle)—

Saddlebags loaded down
With barter—incense, prayer wheels,
And silks—

Instead I met
Not an historical Hun—
But a striking contemporary woman
Who had eyes
The amber colour of dark honey
And high
Cheekbones—
A gentle-hearted, well-spoken woman—
The lady supervisor of our building site—
From Mongolian Foreign
Affairs—

The first to touch my crystal
To her lips,
This Ulan-Bator lady friend's
Name!—Namsraijav—an
Easeful sound!
Like a breath!
The breathing
Of a woman well-spoken who
Worked for

The Foreign Ministry in Ulan-Bator,
And who lived
In a modest place,
The only painting on her walls
Not a Tibetan, but Russian artist-philosopher,
Nikolai Rerikh—a painting
Called the Himalayas

From time to time
Her granddaughter—a small lively girl
Appeared speaking
Mongolian—
There was no way
I could answer, so, learning to
Be a diplomat, I stared out
The window
Seeing nothing but clusters of yurts
Enclosing a concrete
Industrial plaza of
Five-storied, standard, Soviet-style units—

"We have no
Tradition of the
Enclosing
Wall," she said,

"Especially if it's a concrete wall—
Myself,
I have a yurt
In the suburbs."

After a swallow of
A strong
Arkhi
Served by Namsraijav in
Silver
Thimble-cups—
She showed me
Books—

Albums of Buddhist spiritual art
Then—unexpectedly—
A book of
Anna Akhmatova's Poems!
"She is my favourite,
Oh so passionate—
No word of hers is a lie—
A poet with a hard eye,
A woman's heart!—
Oh Vladimir, I am a witness to
Her life—Yes!

I read her words—
Every day:

Neither by boat nor push-
Cart could you have got here
Through ankle-deep water or slush…

Anna,
A widow while still young,
And here is
A book by a man
Murdered by
The Bolsheviks in 1921—
An innovator,
A poet, who was
Her husband—Nikolai Gumilev—
(I hope you know about him),
He helped to invent
Acmeism,
A style in
Russia after the Revolution,
And when
Akhmatova was young
She was an Acmeist."

With a proprietary air,
Namsraijav took down
From the shelf
Several books
And journals—
I read the name of
The son
(Anna Akhmatova
And Nikolai Gumilev)—
Lev Gumilev

Namsraijav looked at me,
A little crook
Of a smile
At the corner
Of her mouth
(It was Christmas Eve,
She drank to me
Only with her eyes
A crystal glass...)

ABOUT HIM

"What would you like
To hear,
Vladimir Pavlovitch,
You—our Soviet architectural ambassador
From Moscow
Here in Ulan-Bator,
So close by
Your construction
Site? How
About Mongolian Buddhism? Or
Our conquerors—
Baty? Genghis Khan?
Tamerlane Timur—
We are a
Fidgety
Nomadic people—so,
How about
HIM?—my
Student friend ?—
WELL—it was
1936! we'd been sent
To Leningrad from Mongolia,
Four or five of us,
The year before
He (Lev) had already been

Expelled once
But he had
Come back to us,
To Leningrad—and
Then there was
The winter purge of 1937
When we were all sent home
Late in the fall
From the University,
Oh, it was so long ago,
January, when he was
Arrested—exactly like the first arrest—
They took him away
On the tail-end of
A blizzard—
Much later, I wrote
Letters to him from
Far off Mongolia
But of course,
He did not answer,
Not from
The Gulag!
Our friendship was
Broken for decades, decades!
Lev
The Lion!

Yes—in his heart he was
A Lion,
A King among wild beasts,
A warrior whose
Outlook and intuitions
Were all rooted
In ethnological
Theory—as a student,
I'd run
Down a
University
Hallway—I'd run out
On a winter's
Rainy day
To listen
To our favourite,
Evgeny Victorovich—
Oh!
Wearing
My funny Mongolian fur hat
And sheep coat!
I was
Soaked through,
A young female animal
From the steppes.
He
Stopped—grasped

My hand—
Looking
At me with
Wide-open eyes!
I was faint
And tried to free my hand
But he laughed loudly and
Cried:
'Oh steppe gazelle!
Oh stone-sculpted
Maiden
Of Siberia!
Oh bride of Genghis Khan,
Borte—
And Khulan!
Oh female wolf from the
River Altai!
Oh Camel! Horse! Coyote!
Oh flying Bird!'"

LENINGRAD

This bright eager
Young girl from
The Soviet border republic of
Mongolia
Had been sent to Leningrad
As a student; it was
A time of post-Revolutionary
Slogans,
The Re-education
And renovation of Soviet life!
New industry, new agriculture!
The poster joy of
Determinedly smiling sloganeering faces,
Soviet Youth And the Youth of the World
On the March!

"Namsraijav! Girl from a
Different far-Eastern race!
Quick. Join us! Help us
Heal our after-Revolutionary
Wounds!
You came to us—
We need your help!
Don't let Russian words frighten you,

You're young—
Fluency will come!"

Her head was in
Mongolia!
"Why are we who we are?
Why is a camel a camel instead of a car?
Why an eagle instead of a plane?
Why do we migrate?
Why do we think our yurts are palaces!
Why so many Whys
And more Whys?
Who's got an answer? Any
Answer?"

And now in Leningrad!
"We had met in the main Hall
Of the Faculty of History
He was himself starry-eyed
And soon he was showing his little
Researcher
How we all—each of us together
And each of us as a nation,
Begin our lives—

"We became friends—
Close enough for me to try to
Understand who he was,
His temperament!—
One day
We were
Laughing out loud
As we burst in from the cold
Into his rooms—

"He stamped his feet
To shake off the snow,
I'd taken no notice but
Oh!—She,
The Queen of Mothers—Oh! there she was,
For real, for a fact—
Anna Akhmatova—

"As I looked in on
The living room, I saw
Bulging bookshelves,
Clusters of photographs on
The walls
And

She was sitting
Cocooned in her own stillness,
The open door—
Her long pale face—
Oblivious
To us, to me—

"My heart skipped
Oh my Mongolian gods!
I was sure, there
And then, that
I had some kind of
Singular
Intimate feel for her mood.
I heard her mezzo voice,
Those honed, hard lines
Written
For her loved son—
Lev Gumilev, my
Co-student:

The past is rotting in the future—
A terrible carnival of dead leaves

"'Today there's no sun,' she said dryly,
Looking at me,
'Only our usual gloom, our snow-bound
Wet winter weather!
So why do you
Squint your eyes?
You won't see our city
Leningrad—
Saint Petersburg—
Any better—not with that squint!
It is impolite—to be
So proud! Namsraijav!
Our little girl
From Mongolia!'

"Oh!—those acerbic words,
Those cutting words,
Cast me back
To Mongolia,
To
My own
Ulan-Bator mother
Who'd seen me off to Leningrad,
Letting out a
Mother's
Howl of admonition—

'No Russian men!
None!
No lily-white
Snow—not in my blood,
Not in my
Grandchildren!'
I'm sorry. That's exactly what she said—

"At Akhmatova's
After she'd looked
Me in the eye like that,
I swung
The door open and
Ran downstairs
From the third
Floor—
Lev bounding after me:
'Namsraijav, Namsraijav! Stop!
Don't be a fool!'
In the distance, through the
Blustering snow
I saw a streetcar!—

"'Namsraijav! Stop! Stop!
My crazy Hun of a Muse!

Stop!...'
His words
Pounding in my
Poor head
Unreal—
Under the
Teasing
Of a streetcar's
Knock knock knocking
Carriage—

"Bitter
Tears—
I could feel them welling
Up in my eyes—
Again I heard
His mother's words—
Her—the Queen
Of Russian poetry:

Don't come crawling like a whelp
Into my bed of loneliness.
I don't know you.

Vladimir Pavlovich,
Let me ask you!
How long since
You have read her?
Here are her spare little books,
Read
Them
In the night when you
Are working on your
Blueprints and
Drafts—
I'm sure her clean hardness of
Line will help
With your drawings."

II

POEMS: ANNA AKHMATOVA

Translated by Vladimir Azarov and Barry Callaghan

I question her: 'And were you Dante's guide,
Dictating the Inferno?' She answered: 'Yes.'
—Anna Akhmatova, "The Muse"

TO ALEXANDER BLOK

I went to see the poet
At exactly twelve noon, Sunday.
It was quiet in the wide room.
Outside, freezing cold.

A raspberry sun
Trailed tatters of blue smoke...
That sun, like my laconic host,
Cast a slant eye on me!

A host whose eyes
No one can forget;
Best be careful,
Don't look into them at all.

But I do recall how we talked
That Sunday noon, how we sat
Smoking in the tall grey house
By the mouth of the Neva.

HE LOVED THREE THINGS...

He loved three things in life:
White peacocks, evensong,
And old maps of America.
He hated hearing a child's strife,
Hate tea with lemon,
And womanish hysteria.
...I was his wife.

UNDER THE ROOF

Nothing stirs under the roof
Of my house. A stillness of hours.
I read the Acts of the Apostles
And Psalms of praise.

We meet, it's wonderful, blue
Stars shine through the ice—
A red maple leaf marks my Bible
At Solomon's Song of Songs.

HOW CAN YOU BEAR TO LOOK...?

How can you bear to look at the Neva?
How can you bear to cross its bridges?
Your footstep is a feverish
Phantom in my heart.
Black angels strop their wings.
The scything dead are on the road
Where a curbside fire grows like a
Crimson rose in the driven snow.

A ROAD

A darkening park-side road
Where lamps bleed yellow light.
Keep calm. Don't goad
Or speak ill of him tonight.

Embraced by time and tears,
We'll kiss, stroll about, and grow
Old as each year disappears
In a swirl of stars made of snow.

I CANNOT SMILE

I cannot smile, ice wind.
Lips sealed with rime.
My only hope has disappeared,
Foretelling this song of mine.

Which I now give to you
To ridicule, to profane,
Your silence in the face
Of my love is unbearable.

CRUCIFIXION

"Weep not for Me, Mother.
I am alive in my grave."

I

Angels in their grief are moaning.
Heaven is on fire and melting.
Unto the Father: "Why hast Thou forsaken...?"
And to the Mother: "Weep no more."

II

Magdalena writhed, Magdalena wept, Lord.
The Belov'd disciple, in his petrified grief, atoned, Lord.
No one dared look, a silence was kept, Lord,
There, where the Mother stood alone, O Lord.

III

LEV GUMILEV

LEV MY LION

Who is Lev
My Lionheart?

You don't seem
To know much about him—

That is no good—
Russians need to know

Who their heroes are:

They never broke him, never mind sixteen years in Stalin's camps,
Never mind his fighting at the Front during WWII,

Or being in a Nazi concentration camp.
He never gave up his love for life,

Or his work, his research, his creativity—
What we know is this,

That after he was convicted a second time in the late 1940s
And sentenced to ten years in the Gulag

For anti-Soviet ideological activities, he continued
Trying to refine his definition of ethnography,

Writing, in sub-zero winters of the camp, most of his
Best-known book—*Ethnogenesis and the Biosphere*—

With the first chill on the air
With the first snow

Settled on their nests
The Birds

Fly they fly!
Pulse through the sky

Flocks in the millions
Caught up in a nomadic need,

Take flight, a need,
A passion for the uprooting of homes—

Tribes side-winding
Across the rolling steppes, the

Dry grass lands—hauling their
Yurts behind them.

It's always been the same blood
Surge, the migratory

Packing up of settlements,
The crossing of boundaries,

Social barriers, bastions—
Always on the move, it's in their hearts—

Why?—
The feral reach for life?

This biosignal, this
Angelic inwit in the marrow,

This constant pulse
In the nomadic mind—

Watch a flock
Bracing against wind

Currents—
Be more attentive

To the emerging ruler, the visionary,
The commandant, the butcher,

The First Infantry Consul,
The First Horseman in the sky—

Genghis Khan, Odegei Khan,
Guyuk Khan, Baty Khan,

Monuke Khan, Kublai Khan—
Lenin, Stalin, Lucifer—

Jesus Christ Superstar!
Buddha among the birds!

And behind
Each leader—infected by

The Virus—
Infected by the blood surge

(Lev Gumilev's insight),
Passion as a vehicle—

The readiness to fight—to free captives or to fetter slaves,
To fight for the Word, for water, spices, the Virgin, oil,

Oh!—the whistling
Arrow of Love &

War, poetry for Othello, poetry for the
Khans!

Passion's rapacious contour that
Runs counter to life on behalf of life.

PASSION THEORY

He was the son of two

Prominent Petrograd or
Leningrad poets—

—Lev Gumilev—

A Soviet dissident,
An outspoken academician

Whose unorthodox ideas about
The birth and death of

Groups came
To be known as

Neo-Eurasianism—
A new Ethnology!

—Lev Gumilev—

Took, as his basis, historic and philosophic theories

Rejected by almost everyone in his time—he was the father of
Theatrical ethnogenesis, according to which nations originate out
Of the predictable paradigms of societal development

"Passion" being a man's hereditary biological ability to create in
His "passion-field" his own history

Prophet Mohammed, Alexander of Macedonia, Napoleon, Vladimir Lenin.

"Passionarity" being a level of vital surging energy—

A power characteristic within an ethnic group
That causes men to pass on through stages of

Development, climax, inertia, convolution, and memory

Even when, as was the case with Europe then,
The person or group was in a state of deep inertia—

A "state" Gumilev called our period of
"Introduction to obscuration."—He believed that

Oriental culture and Western civilization had
Merged on their way through Russia, one piggybacking

On the other, and he asked us to understand, in this context,
How and why civilization and culture are not the same

Civilization being the use of the results of culture—
Culture being a movement through thousands of generations

CLOSE TO THE CEILING

Midsummer—
The blistering Ulan-Bator sun is blotted by

A dry sand-filled wind,
Normal for the season!

Namsraijav showed up at the
Building site—

Being inside, I had no idea what the weather
Was like, I was working up close to the

Ceiling—
"Hey Vladimir!—

We're going to Gandan today,
Where a monk's waiting for us"—

She's looking up—I've got my hands full of
Fabrication orders

For an acoustic
Drop ceiling—

Going over construction drawings made by my
Main partner—the

Finnish group, NOKIA, in
Particular a dozen

Crystal chandeliers coming
From Austria

Dangerously heavy—but there I am,
Hovering in future space—nose

To the ceiling—suspended—in preparation
For that evening's gathering of

Solemn suits, triangles of snow-white shirts set
Between black satin tuxedo lapels,

The scent of eau de cologne—the rustle of
Silk gowns, chiffon and satin—

Oh beaming ladies!
But in the future future future!

I am up here!—oh!
Namsraijav:

"Vladimir! Vladimir!
We are in a hurry!

The monk insists on punctuality,
Even more than the diplomats!"

And so we walked at a quick pace
Through Choibalsan Square, the Mausoleum—

Then, down clustered alleyways where Chinese
Peasants were selling vegetables from their stalls,

Bright orange carrots, purple beets,
Purple eggplants, green onions—

My question: "Chinese?" and my answer:
"Mongolians seem to have no tradition of

Agriculture; their passion is
Animals—even on the outskirts of town

There are only herds
Of sheep, horses, camels?"

Hills of grey yellow
Grass, ger huts, a nettling wind

(I was wearing short sleeves,
Summer shorts) —

Namsraijav, in a hurry—was
Short of breath—

"Never mind, we'll rest,
We'll go into the library,

You'll see the Sacred Books in
Several scripts—

Be patient—
I'll give you a little talk

On our history—
All the changes—the language—

The—
Our great GANDAN...

Oh Vladimir—
We need to stop and rest but

We're still a half-hour away!
Never mind. Let's sit, open the water

Bottle on this knoll, and
Read:"

Our oldest surviving literary work
Was written for the Mongol royal family after Genghis Khan's death

In AD 1227—in the Uyghur script—it is the single
Most significant native Mongolian account of Genghis Khan

As it provides the richest source for pre-Classical Mongolian
And Middle Mongolian usage—and also

POETRY in the PHAGS-PA LAMA SCRIPT—

An alphabet designed by the Tibetan Lama Zhogoin Qoigyai Pagba
(PHAGS-PA LAMA) for Yuan emperor Kublai Khan

Used widely for only about a hundred years during
The Yuan Dynasty—it fell out of favour with the advent of the Ming Dynasty

*The Uyghur-based Mongolian alphabet is not a perfect fit for Middle
Mongolian, and it would be impractical to extend it to a language with
a very different phonology like Chinese. Therefore, during the Yuan
Dynasty (ca. 1269), Kublai Khan asked Phags-pa to design a new*

alphabet for use by the whole empire. Phags-pa extended his native Tibetan script (an Indic script) to encompass Mongol and Chinese, evidently Central Plains standard. The resulting thirty-eight letters have been known by several descriptive names, such as "square script" based on their shape, but today are primarily known as the Phags-pa alphabet. Despite its origin, the script was written vertically (top to bottom) like the previous Mongolian scripts. It did not receive wide acceptance and fell into disuse with the collapse of the Yuan Dynasty in 1368. After this it was mainly used as scripts on Tibetan currency in the twentieth century, as script for Tibetan seal inscriptions from the Middle Ages up to the twentieth century and for inscriptions on the entrance doors of Tibetan monasteries. Unlike the ancestral Tibetan script, all Phags-pa letters are written in temporal order and in-line.

"Are you okay?—I know
It's hard reading all that—

Come on—we've rested up—
Get ready for a Holy Sacrament!"

And an unexpected
Whirl of wind brings

Grey clouds and
Large drops of rain plopping down on us.

Namsraijav has brought an umbrella to ward off the sun
I lean against her under it—

Through the pummeling sound of water
I hear

Bells—light but still solemn—
The cautious chimes of someone in hiding

Or of birds splashing
Amidst a rustle of wings

Then the sun has broken out again
Over the back end of the city where the

Hills roll away into a
Copper-coloured monotony

But around us, cupolas,
Yurts, ger huts,

Camels, horses,
Cars, here

In the Empire of the Holy surviving GANDAN—
Silhouette of the temples

The oldest Buddhist Monastery in Mongolia!—

Small mobile monasteries of the nomad people functioned in Mongolia, and in 1838 the Gandantegchinlen Monastery was founded as the religious centre of Sutra-Tantra Buddhism at the site of Dalkha hill. It grew into a complex of colleges including a college of basic Buddhist teachings, departments of Astrology and Medicine, and as such was the largest centre of Mongolian Buddhism. The first temple of the Monastery was built at the initiative of the Mongolian living Buddha, the Fifth Incarnation Bogdo, Chultem-Jigmid-Dambijantsan. It was constructed by Mongolian masters and made mostly of wood and earth following Mongolian national architectural designs, with gold-plated roofs and topmost Buddhist symbolic—decorations. Many of the Bodhisattvas statues and images established in Gandan temple are of significance. In the temple there are a bronze statue of the Lofty Nobel Rimpoche Dzanabazar—the Mongolian living Buddha of the First Incarnation sculpted by himself at the behest of his mother; the collection of the Buddha's fundamental teachings, the Tripitaka (Gangiur) in one hundred and eight volumes; the silver statue of the famous Tsong (Khapa) of Amdo made in XVI century in Western Oirat Mongolia. In 1938, the communists suppressed religious communities in Mongolia. They destroyed around nine hundred monasteries, though a handful were turned into museums. The monks were killed, jailed, or forced to join the army or laity. Five temples of Gandan Monastery were destroyed. The remaining temples were used to accommodate Russian officials or used as barns to keep their horses. In 1944, after a petition from several monks, Gandan Monastery was reopened but its functions were carried out under the strict supervision of the socialist government. There are currently ten datsans and temples operating at Gandan Monastery, and approximately nine hundred monks.

TAMERLANE

"Hey! Hey!
Who's disturbing

My sacred deep—(several hundred
Year) sleep!

These fools
They call archeologists!

WHOEVER DARES TO DISTURB THIS TOMB
WILL BRING THE DEMONS OF WAR ONTO THE LAND

Stop your mad digging!
Hands off

No embalming
My body—

I'm sleeping the
Sleep of human stubbornness!

I cannot stop you?
Oh! oh! oh!

That Soviet anthropologist!
June 1941!

Three days later
The Nazis invaded

Operation Barbarossa!
Millions dead—

Leading to the
Necessary destruction of

Germany!
Ha Ha Ha Ha! that's how it goes!

Just ask me, Tamerlane,
My bones re-interred

Some things
Are best left alone!"

The Mongolian Buddhist Golden Horde of the thirteenth-fourteenth century was replaced by the Islamic Timurid empire in the fifteenth century. Its leader was TAMERLANE—the Central Asian conqueror, known as Timur, from the Turkish word for "Iron." Through intelligence, military skill and thrust of personality, Timur conquered an empire that stretched from Russia to India, and from the Mediterranean Sea to Mongolia. Unlike Genghis Khan, however, Timur conquered not to open trade routes but to loot and pillage. The Timurid Empire did not long survive its founder; he had seldom bothered to put any kind of governmental structure in place once he'd destroyed the existing order. Tamerlane was also known as a great patron of the arts, literature and architecture. One of his signal achievements was his capital, the beautiful city of Samarkand, first city of the Islamic world.

IV

MONGOLIAN ÉTUDES

WHY CAMELS ROLL IN ASHES

Back when Boghan named the animals
And eleven of the twelve months of the Mongolian

Calendar, there were two animals left
The CAMEL and the RAT

They fought over who should be the twelfth

Boghan did not want either to become upset,
Saying they would have to settle

The problem on their own
The Camel and the Rat made a bet that whoever

Saw the sun first on the following morning
Would win. The Camel stood facing the east

Waiting while the Rat mounted the Camel's humps
And fixed his gaze on the mountains

When the rising Sun flooded across the Mountain range
The Rat was first to see the light

The Camel was so upset at losing the bet
He tried to stomp the Rat to death

The Rat however ran and hid under a pile of ashes
Now it is said that

Whenever a CAMEL sees dead fires of any kind
He wreaks revenge on his enemy the RAT

By stomping and rolling about in the ashes—

INTERMISSION

Namsraijav all smiles—closed the
Coloured book and said to

Her bounding granddaughter:
"Our next lesson will be Pushkin—

His Fairy Tales!—remember?—yesterday
We read The Sleeping Beauty—

My small princess of Ulan-Bator—
Tomorrow—

We will read Ruslan and Ludmila
About the Smart Russian Cat

On the Golden Chain—I will
Tell you even more Fairy Tales!

You are so tired—
So sleepy, like Pushkin's Beauty!"

KHAN AKHMAT

(Namsraijav's joyful sonnets!)

Hey Vladimir! You do not know—
Great Akhmatova Had Our
Mongol
Blood!— Listen
To what she wrote: "Khan Akhmat
My ancestor—was killed
One night in his tent
By a Russian
Thug
And Karamzin

Says in his
History
Of the Russian State
That
This killing
Marked the lifting of the Mongol
Yoke from the neck of Russia—it was known
That this Akhmat was a Descendant
Of Genghis Khan!..."

So it was that she passed on to
Her son Lev her genes
That bore
A love for
Nomadic
People!

MODIGLIANI

(Amedeo's poem to Anna)

> *A deception that elevates us*
> *is dearer than a host of truths.*
> —MARINA TSVETAEVA

Your apparition amidst my ennui—Anna
Your exquisite silhouette—Anna
Your perfect profile behind my painted women—Anna
Your murmuring of unknown words in my ear—Anna

Your serpent touch an electric jolt
Your thin wrists braceleted by rapture
Your palm, your porcelain fingers
Long-stemmed flowers splayed on my chest

The holes in your white Venetian mask blessed by your eyes—
Green in the morning like the green of your Black Sea,
Black in the night like the black veil of your green Baltic
Saint Petersburg shrouded by freezing rain—

You, pale icon, are my purgatorial prayer—Anna
You, pale icon, are my first misfortune in love—Anna

The poem is based on the Parisian love affair between Amedeo Modigliani & Anna
Akhmatova, who had recently married; after a year, Anna returned to her husband.

BY THE BAY BY THE SEA...

At my window after
Namsraijav's visit on a deep indigo night
Lit up by
Houses across the street...

At hand, Pushkin's *By the Bay by the Sea*
My new friend Namsraijav makes
Me restless.
I don't need distraction,

Not now, not at this crucial moment—
From the window I can
See the wide Mongolian night sky,

The street below
My third floor window
Dimly lit—
A sallow lamplight—
Sparse

Trees, hydro poles,
Idling cars—
Namsraijav's reading
Is on my mind—

Tomorrow's homeschooling Russian class
For her small girl during which a Smart Cat
Will tell Stories!—
I open my Pushkin book—

By the Bay by the Sea... and know
Deep in my bones that
I am not in my own country,

Ulan-Bator is
1300 meters above mean
Sea level—too high
For me—

Too hard on my blood pressure!
Every morning, a well-polished
Diplomatic
Chaika limousine—
Small red flag fluttering—

Takes me
For my
Needle—
Magnesia!

Oh! the mortification—an
Execution every morning!

I do not need to bare
My modest ass in Ulan-Bator—

Oh! the pointillism of it all!
Hey!—turn the page—*By the Bay by the Sea...*
Those blueprints and drawings due yesterday
Can wait—as I read:

A.S. PUSHKIN

Ruslan and Ludmila
Prologue

(my loose translation)

By the Bay by the Sea—a Green Oak grows
A Gold Chain threaded through its dense foliage
A Cat—Very Smart—is walking around
The Oak and up and down from
Link to Link in the Chain—
If Cat goes right, he sings Songs
If he goes left, he tells Fairy Tales—
Oh!—this is all Wonderful—a Wood-Goblin out for a stroll;

Rusalka sits in the Oak's branches;
There are Traces of Unseen Beasts
On Unknown Paths;
There is a Hut that's unsteady
Stuck up on Chicken Legs
No Windows or Doors—
The Wood and Dale are full of Visions—
Sunrise comes accompanied by Splashing Waves
On the Sand
Shore—an empty beach
Except for a long train of
Thirty Warriors who've come up out of the Sea
Where the King's Son, a Knight, captures
A brutal tyrant—the Harsh Tsar;
Beyond the Woods, beyond the Seas
And through the Clouds the Evil Sorcerer
Flees with the vanquished Knight;
Princess cries in a Dark Keep
Wolf is her loyal Servant;
On a sturdy Broom a Wicked Witch takes off
Through the night sky for no reason;
The Immortal Tsar Katshey
Bent beneath the weight of Gold
Is looking for Russian Souls—
I was There and tasted the Honey!
I saw an Oak—wonderful and green!
I sat in the shade while Real Smart the Cat

Told me magic Stories of inspiration—
And I remember One—
MONGOLIAN ÉTUDES!

ANATOLI TSHEGLOVSKI

Namsraijav put on a silk shawl:

"No—I did not know him—
My white grandfather—
Just a couple of blurred photographs
In the old wooden box kept in one
Of our yurts—
I did not feel white blood in my veins—
The sun of Mongolia's short
Summer gives me warmth,
My energy—
My intuitions—dare I say—
I derive who I am
From our noble Khans—I feel it—
Not from him—Anatoli Tsheglovski!
That Polish Pan!—
A soldier in the Tsarist Army
Between two eras—before the First War
Maybe earlier?
My grandmother brought him from the taiga
To our quiet homeland—he was a Polish patriot,
He deserted
As a Russian officer near Warsaw, where he
Was caught and sent to the outback
Of the Urals

To East Siberia
This was when Polish deserters
Were jailed near the town of Yekaterinburg—
Travelling on the Trans-Siberian Railway
He jumped from the roof of the prison car
Into the taiga
And began his long life in the wild wood—
Becoming a local legend!
My mother said his eyes
Were two transparent stones
Two steel arrows
Two electrical currents so strong
They could bring a wolf or a bear to a dead halt
They were his weapon in the taiga
Better than a knife
His weapon in
The schismatic Russian village
He lived outside of, hiding in the woods
In the taiga
For two or three years—
Not talking to people—his Polish accent
An invitation to Russian arrest—
Rain, snow, beasts or predatory birds,
Were his life—since he was afraid of people—
Any noise in the brush was a signal
Of Russians on the hunt, out to capture him—
On the run in the endless taiga!

Then he met a woman—almost a girl
Who had kind narrow eyes—he liked her accent—
He felt her warmth

Why do you want to go to Mongolia?

She asked Pan Anatoli Tsheglovski—

I like your talk and your narrow eyes—
They are so different—they are not hard like mine—
They are dark like the night and they ask me
To love you!"

SELF-PORTRAIT

Rising from the past, my shadow
Is running in silence to meet me.
—ANNA AKHMATOVA

A loud clanging signals
A twenty minute secondary school break—
Unsmiling women
Behind a griddle are baking

Thin rounds of dark bread
And little cakes covered by lashings of jam

Biting into this pastry I try to
Dream of being back in Leningrad, not
Here in Kazakhstan, where I am an alien—

But I remember nothing
Except fog, leaden rainy clouds, ruined
Spires from WWII

Headless sculptures—
A loud toneless clang—
The bell of a streetcar—

In the back seat—a girl sits—

She covers her weeping with her hands—
Her face is so familiar—

I cry out—"Why are you in Leningrad—while
I am here—in your land of Mongolia!
Let's swap places!"—
The girl stops crying—"Ah! you are

Namsraijav my Muse—
Disappeared one autumn—"
An Index Finger—embraced by

An Aristocratic Lady's brilliant ring, points
To a girl————I don't know this
Proud woman—I just remember Words—
Namsraijav shudders————the teacher's voice:

"Yes—Words—Vladimir! please, repeat
After me!" "I am sorry!" and I hear,
I see:
"The Golden Horde,

Bows and arrows, swords—hurtling by horse
Over the barren steppes
Into soil-rich Europe,

GENGHIS KHAN the advance-guard..."
I see Him—the great Khan—

I see Him in my mind,
Our great leader Stalin's spitting image—
And to my surprise!
Genghis Khan the Great

Winds a Gold Chain around
Pushkin's Oak—green and close by the Bay—
Retelling *Mongolian Études*
In place of Alexander Sergeevich!

For whom? for me? No
For this small girl?—Oh! she is
Namsraijav's granddaughter
Named Khulan—named as if she were a new bride—
For Genghis Khan

Time flies—an end-of-the-line streetcar trip—
Namsraijav gets off—
Her daughter is sitting near her daughter
The small girl named—remember? Khulan—
They hold a book—WHAT?

It is *Mongolian Études*!

I'd recently sent it to them—
And behind this family klatch
There's Genghis Khan—HIMSELF!—
Smiling approval—lip-syncing English...

VESTIBULARITY

"Why are you standing there
Looking at me so sadly?"
He asked lying on the bed—
He being my father—
It was so long ago
After he'd got
Out of the Gulag
In the early 60s when,
As a student,
I spent my university vacation
With my family—
"Why are you standing there
Looking at me so sadly?"
Still half-asleep
He turned to me
In a cold sweat,
Wetting the pillow,
His hair tangled.
 "Oh—my crazy dizziness!
Everything's topsy-turvy,
Spinning in circles!
I always had a problem with
My vestibular apparatus
Always—
It's why I never did fly

ared
hundred and fifty hours—
st a hundred and twenty"—
But I knew the truth—I knew why
He had not finished his
Flight training—he'd been expelled
Because of politics
From the aeronautical school—
Oh! fly fly fly young man!
You are still a pilot!
Listen like a doctor
To the beating of
Your metal heart
You are our up-and-coming aircraft designer!
Fly fly fly
This is the new
Soviet world
Of the Science of the Skies.
Defeat!—that's what we want,
The defeat of all our enemies
The enemies of the world Proletariat!
The curse of my father's dizziness
Was never spoken:
A political secret from back in his young life,
His brain's whirling turbulence
As Stalin looped-the-loop—

I relived, in part,
His heritage:
      WHEN—
I spent a terrible five hours
Airsick
Flying from Moscow to Mongolia,
To Ulan-Bator—
So that I took the five-day long
Trans-Siberian Rail
When I went back—

In Russia it lasted for four years
WWII was over—
We were still living
In Kazakhstan—
When capitalist America, with a kind of slapdash cunning,
Held out a helping hand:
And—down the crooked Kazakh
Potholed roads
Came agile Willyses and
Noisy Studebakers—
We boys chased after
This new auto-technology!

How come I remember this now—
So far from my
Kazakh boyhood?
Here in Mongolia,
With mostly Ulan-Bator on my mind—
But still, I do remember—
A powder in a little box
That had the
Heartbreaking smell of
Vanilla!
My mother made this

For me—a dessert—a
Soft porridge called a pudding!

Oh! such memories
Of UNCLE SAM! who seemed to come
In all sizes—
As we were given gifts of clothing
Second-Hand—
All of us! the whole population of
Our settlement!
(And probably for all of
Post-war Russia!)
Second-Hand but
So beautiful! and almost new—
Uncle Sam who wore
Thousands of coats, suits,
Shoes (male and female), dresses,
(Of an indeterminate sex), underwear (where the sex
Was obvious!),
Scarves, jeans, gloves, socks—
I remember
A fluffy camel's hair beige smoking jacket
With a silk brown collar—perfect for
Sitting beside a fireplace with a Havana cigar—
(Not that I'd ever smoked a cigar)
My father had smoked a Russian Belomor

n the Gulag—
(On TV TSM the same smoking jacket
Was worn by Cary Grant!)
My crafty mother made
Me a winter coat
From the camel's hair jacket
To ward off the Kazakh blizzards—
So there I was, a beige furry figure
Surviving swirls
Of driven snow
Thanks to the warmth
Of Uncle Sam—the Second-Hand Man.

SHORT ON WORDS

He was—
Reticent, laconic—
My father—
He came out of the
Gulag camps and
Told me almost nothing about
His hellish years there—
A couple of
Words about
His only pal—
How they had
Helped
Each other—
To
Survive—and once—
About another friend—
A girl—
A student
From the fog-bound canals of
His beloved
Leningrad—
My father and the girl and the camp—
All he said was
She had reached out to touch
A high voltage wire

"With her little girl fingers"—
Short on words
My father was—

MY NKVD VISIT: GOING HOME

> *Can I see another's grief,*
> *And not seek for kind relief?*
>> —WILLIAM BLAKE, "Songs of Innocence"

A foggy day
The end of winter—I am only
Two days old
I am Vladimir!
And I am now about six months old
I am in the arms of
My young mother who is walking
The slushy sidewalks of Leningrad—
I am happy with my mother's milk
When she has time to feed me—

My mother, walking rapidly, almost running, this future Soviet
Judge who passionately dreams of bringing the enemies of the
Soviet people to heel, to Justice

Yes! she's in a hurry—
She needs to meet with
The NKVD
Because my father has been
Arrested in the night—why?
There's been all kinds of misdirection

confusion

our young Socialist State—
A new honest powerful authority has
Problems!
Hurry hurry, mother! help
My father!
Help the NKVD do their holy
Work, help them avoid
Mistakes to
Reach the shining peaks of
Communism!

The door is closed behind us. I see a nice man who looks at me, smiles,
Clucks his tongue! I am smiling at him, hearing his sweet speech:

"You cannot know this, you—
Trusting daughter of our democratic life—
The chameleon mask of our enemies is so dark
Maybe he—that is, your former husband,
Was drawn into an anti-Soviet conspiracy
Against his will—but now he is our
Real enemy—no one who is innocent
Is arrested and sent to trial! yes! yes!
Yes! and please stop! you are—
Naïve!
Stop—you foolish girl!"

His face flushes red!—I certainly do not know what to do at
Young age! Cry? The man is now hysterical. I am listening to
Him shout:

"Stop—stupid girl!—you fool!
You?—are you a future Soviet judge?
Our future seer? defender of
Socialism? Communism?!
Stop! he is an enemy!
Yes! he! he! he! your husband!
He is on the other side! he's a traitor! a renegade!
A fifth column!
I'm trying to open your blind eyes!
Forget him, go to the University
Get your Judicial Diploma!
You are so energetic, smart!
You could help us!
Hey! listen! you are different—
Your new husband—he is here!—
Waiting for you in the hallway!"

WHAT?! in her silence—she—my mother—lays me down on
The NKVD table—I am surprised—I wait, lying on the secret
Papers of the NKVD—without a word my mother goes to him!
To the NKVD man—and—she S-L-A-P-S! his clean-shaven
Pink cheek! so very very hard!—I shudder, peeing into my
Russian nappy—oh poor kid!—my time to cry!

.n very happy!
am already one year old! I hear
The lulling clacking sound of the carriage wheels!
I am sitting on
A small square table by the train window
A metal spoon *pings* in the tea glass
The tea is cold
The naked early spring landscape flashes by—
Leningrad—
To the far East!
A long long long way—days days days
So many days
To Kazakhstan!

In the icy storm countryside of Kazakhstan a tall and not-too-
Young Man appears—almost two years old! I can speak. I ask
My mother: WHO IS THIS MAN?

Your father!
He has come to us—under appeal, he
Has exchanged his
Leningrad jail cell for
Kazakhstan in exile—
And later—as a schoolboy you will
Read in Russian history:
Pushkin's revolutionary friends—they were
Called Decembrists—tried to effect

A revolution in Saint Petersburg
In the early nineteenth century—tried to overthrow
The Tsar, wanting a Republic, a Parliament!—
They were exiled to Siberia—noble men—
And their aristocratic loving wives went
With them into that cold wild land!
So your father has repeated history—he has
Come to us in Kazakhstan—"

ON THE ORIGIN OF EVERGREENS

Since Erleg Khaan
Brought Disease into the world

Men, grown old, grew sick and died
Raven, however, took pity on mankind

He was determined to restore all humanity
To its immortality

A huge mountain, Humber Ula, rose up at the centre
Of the world. Upon a high peak

An Aspen, thick with leaves all golden,
Stood beside a crystal clear spring,

The spring of Life, and whoever drank
From its waters had health and a life forever.

Raven flew to the SPRING of Life.
He took up water in his beak, as much as he could,

Intending to carry that water to the whole of humanity
So that, with a few drops, they would be immortal again.

As he flew down to EARTH
He neared a grove beside mankind's camp.

An OWL cried out from the trees—
RAVEN, startled, opened his beak,

Water spilled over all the PINES
And this is why PINE trees are forever green

While the leaves of other trees—like man—
Grow old, fragile, and drop off, to Die.

EPILOGUE

FROST, SO CRISP

Frost, so crisp
Rose white blue snow

And ice smooth as glass
So many holes

Drilled straight down by my
Fishermen friends

Who love the dance of freshly caught fish
The slapping tails

The quivering of those
Who dream of diving back down through

Black holes bored by
My fellow craftsmen, who

Make me feel my own failure,
My rod, my hook,

Empty, no twisting beast's joyful
Dance,

The sky emptying, from cold
Rose into an evening teal blue,

The corpse-de-ballet scaled and quartered, blood

The men laughing, blood, putting in a sack
All the severed parts for their wives.

"Come! You'll help us clean up the blood and eat!
We've got too much for our own tables!"

NAMSRAIJAV OCHIR
MEETINGS AND MEMOIRS
(Lev Gumilev, Anastasiya Tsvetaeva, Yury Rerikh)

Translated by Christopher Barnes

We present the memoirs of Namsraijav Ochir (1915–2004), who was a well-known participant in the international women's movement. She was born in Mongolia, but spent almost twenty years of her life in the Soviet Union during the country's most difficult period —the time of the Second World War and the Stalinist repressions. After the War, Namsraijav Ochir returned to Ulan-Bator, where she worked in the civil service and assisted in the development of Mongolia's diplomatic relations with Japan and China.

Namsraijav Ochir lived a long and unusual life, and her fate was closely bound up with the culture of Russia. She knew many members of the Russian intelligentsia, among them were several high-ranking Soviet leaders, major scholars, and diplomats. She was friends with Lev Nikolayevich Gumilev,[1] Anastasiya Ivanovna Tsvetaeva,[2] Yury Nikolayevich Rerikh,[3] Nina Petrovna Tupoleva[4] (sister-in-law of the famous aircraft constructor), and others.

The memoirs were first written down in Ulan-Bator in 2001 and were later added to by Namsraijav herself. We also have letters between Namsraijav and the scholar Lev Gumilev. The letters to Gumilev are preserved in the latter's own apartment-museum in Saint Petersburg, and several of them are printed below as an appendix to the memoirs.

•   •   •

127

a long time ago, before WWII. In summer of the several people were sent from Mongolia to Saint (then known as Leningrad). It was at that time that special graduate studentships were set up for Mongolians. ere were not so many of us—four, to be exact. They were: Tsend Damdinsuren, Gombojav, myself, and one other person. In the first year of our stay, of course, we studied Russian and the basics of Marxism-Leninism. One of us, Gombojav, had previously studied in Paris and in Germany (at that time Mongolians were sometimes sent to these countries), and he had become accustomed to the Parisian way of life. At our classes in Marxism-Leninism he was always asking questions like "But can I go out onto the street and shout: 'Down with Soviet rule!'?" We were terribly afraid and began kicking him under the table to make him be quiet. But he said, "Well, it's natural. In Paris, for example, you can do that sort of thing. But can you do it here or not?" Our instructor was horrified and could not give him an answer. He could not say, "No, you can't do that..." The new, Stalin Constitution had just then come out. That was how our studies went. Then came the year 1937, and of course, Gombojav, who kept asking questions all the time, was arrested and dispatched to faraway Siberia, where he died. As for the others, they never asked any questions, they never spoke out of turn, and they all therefore survived.

At that time the president of the Academy of Sciences was Vladimir Leontyevich Komarov. He also headed the Mongolian Commission and often met with us. In general, there were very many remarkable scholars at that time. For instance, Kazakevich, who was a prominent authority on Mongolian studies. There was Tseveen Jamsran who lived in Leningrad; we knew him very well and often visited him. In addition, there were the geologist Zoya

Lebedeva, Pyotr Stengachkovsky, and Ivan Petrovich Rachkovsky, who were well-known scholars at that time, and there was also Aleksandr Nikolayevich Samoilovich, the director of the Institute of Oriental Studies... In short, these were all highly interesting people. And there was also the Library of the Academy of Sciences to which we often went. Once in the catalogue I found a book entitled *The Dark Faith, or the Shamanism of the Mongolians, and other articles by Dorzhi Banzarov* published in 1891 and edited by Grigory Potanin. We had heard about the scholar Banzarov, who graduated from Kazan University in 1847, but none of us had ever held his book in our hands; there was no copy of it in Mongolia. So I decided to make a copy of the book. I went to the library every day, took the book out and very quickly transcribed it. In this way I made a copy of the whole book.

Once when I was sitting there and copying, in came Lev Gumilev. He was at that time a handsome young man with grey eyes. He saw me sitting there.

"Are you copying that book?" he asked. "I'm studying in the Historical Faculty of the University, and I'm also very interested in the history of Mongolia. I know this book, I've been reading it... When do you think you'll be finished?"

"Well, I think quite soon," I answered. Like myself, Lev Gumilev came to the library every day, and he and I were always talking and walking around in the University area.

At that time, Mongolian graduate students worked according to their own individual study plans. On orders from either Professor Jamsran or else Academician Komarov (I don't recall exactly) I was sent to see the Director of the Hermitage, Professor Leon Orbeli. He received me very courteously and gave orders to issue me with a pass for the museum—I was to acquaint myself with the exhibits from Noyon Uul, which had been brought back from an expedition led by Pyotr Kozlov. I went to the Hermitage every day and examined the Noyon Uul exhibits. But either out of naïveté, or maybe stupidity, not uncommon when we are young, I very quickly ceased taking an interest in Noyon Uul and resumed my visits to the Academy of Sciences' Library, in order to finish copying out Banzarov's book.

Lev Gumilev and I resumed our meetings, walking along the University Embankment, and we once even visited the Kunstkamera.[5] We walked along some of the lanes, recalling Dostoevsky, who had also maybe strolled along these same streets... We talked a lot about Pushkin, since the centenary of his death was approaching. Once (this was in November of 1936), Gumilev said to me, "You know, I'm very much in love with you..." But I was young and stupid, and I answered that I didn't know whether this was allowed... that we were studying Marxism-Leninism here, and the Russian language, and I didn't know what to say to him. Then he repeated, "I love you, Namsraijav, and I'm writing a long poem about you. I'll send you the dedication of the poem through the mail." Soon I received this "Dedication." At that time we were living on the so-called Petrograd Side of Leningrad, in the Academy of Sciences' Graduate Students' Home, and it was there that Gumilev sent his dedication to me—or, rather, in fact it was a whole packet of verses. Unfortunately they have not survived. In April of 1938 when my close friends were arrested, everything was confiscated, including the "Dedication" to Lev Gumilev's poem, and also my portrait painted in 1932 in Moscow by the Russian artist Vasily Belyaev. Only a few lines of the "Dedication" have remained in my memory.

In order not to be forever gloomy,
So as to be more cheerful and tender...
In order that for a moment you recall
My song and my longing,
I'm returning this reflection
Of your foreign beauty...

When we met up again, he asked me, "Did you receive what I sent?"

"Yes," I answered, " I did receive it."

"You know," he said, "I'm writing a whole poem about you. When I finish it, I'll send it to you..." Soon after that, however, Gumilev was arrested. At that time he was in his fourth year of study.

For many years there was no news of him. The two of us met up again only in 1970 in Moscow. At our meeting, Natalya Viktorovna, Gumilev's wife, told me, "You know, he's the sort of man who loves only one woman, and all his life he loved only you. Did you know that? And now he's very glad that he's met you again."

He also told his mother, Anna Akhmatova, that he was in love with a woman from Mongolia. My name is Namsraijav, which is a very complicated, Tibetan name. Akhmatova asked what they called this Mongolian woman, and he told her, "She's called Namsraijav." And Akhmatova said, "Lyovushka, but what a strange name!" Lev Nikolayevich later told his wife about this, and she subsequently recounted the incident to me.

Then Natalya Viktorovna went out and left the two of us alone, and we told one another about what had happened to us over the past thirty-odd years. We remembered our meetings in the year 1936, and Lev Nikolayevich said, "If we had got married just then, we would have had children... When I returned to Leningrad, I tried many times to seek you out and find you. I asked various Mongolians, but they couldn't tell me anything." But our Mongolians in Leningrad did tell me that some person kept constantly asking about me. I asked them to give him my postal address, but nobody took the trouble to do this, and we were not destined to meet or correspond until the 1970s.

In 1972 I sent Lev Nikolayevich a private invitation. Whenever I invited him to come to Mongolia, he always wrote back saying, "Sofiya Vlasyevna will not allow me to go..." I am sure you can guess the meaning of this—"Sofiya Vlasyevna" meant *Sovetskaya vlast'* [the Soviet regime]. And that was how things stood. He was not allowed to leave the country. So we only corresponded. On the 28 August 1972 he wrote to me:

> *I realize that I've lost my way forever*
> *In empty crossings of space and time,*
> *But my native rivers still flow to a place*
> *Where the road is forever barred to me.*

We eventually met once again in Leningrad in 1982. Gumilev then lived in a communal apartment on Kolomenskaya Street. Lev Nikolayevich again regretted that we had not got married in 1936, and I feebly tried to explain that, at that time in any case, they would not have permitted us to marry... He gave me two photographs of himself. That was our last meeting. But we wrote to one another. Lev Nikolayevich sent me his articles and books with touching inscriptions. On the book *The Discovery of Khazaria*

[*Otkrytie Khazarii*] he wrote: "*In memory of our bright meeting in 1936 on the eve of dear Namsraijav's great troubles, from the author.*" On the book *The Quest for the Imaginary Kingdom* [*Poiski vymyshlennogo tsarstva*] he wrote "*To the golden sheet lightning Namsraijav Ochir from an offshoot of the Western Mongols, who has not forgotten the valour of his ancestors. Arslan* [i.e., Lev, or Lion]." On the book *The Huns in China*, he wrote "*To the Eastern Star Namsraijav Ochir. Arslan (Lev).*" And on all the other books that I received from him there were similar inscriptions.

In May of 1992, on returning from a trip to London, I phoned up Saint Petersburg. Lev Nikolayevich was already very ill. He said, "My days are numbered. I've sent you a letter..." In that final letter Lev Nikolayevich wrote: "*I have loved you very greatly. You should know this, since I can see the end coming. Your faithful Arslan. I kiss your hands, Lev Gumilev.*"

When I first got to know Lev Nikolayevich, I was twenty. We became very close friends. But I was from Mongolia, which at that time was considered a foreign country, and we Mongolians were told that we must conduct ourselves modestly when abroad...

I have to say that I have been fortunate in this life. I have seen so many interesting people, starting with Lev Davidovich Trotsky. I came to Russia in 1929. This was at the end of NEP [the New Economic Policy]. We lived at that time "in the manner established by Trotsky." Stalin had at that time not yet appeared, and Trotsky dominated the thoughts and minds of young people. We often saw him on the square. At that time everything was simple. There were no bodyguards. Like all people, the so-called leaders simply walked around on the streets like everyone else. I was sent to study at MOPSh, the Moscow Experimental Model School named after Kalinin, where the son of Maria Kudasheva, wife of Romain Rolland, studied. Also pursuing his studies along with us was a nephew of Vladimir Ilyich [Lenin].

There was a certain man called Grigory Naumovich Voitinsky, an old revolutionary. His wife Maria Kuznetsova had spent a lot of time interned in tsarist prisons, or dungeons as we call them, and she was sick with tuberculosis. In tsarist Russia, Voitinsky had been given a capital sentence, and he fled to America via Siberia. After the February Revolution he returned. And it was their family that now brought me up. They were splendid people. Voitinsky used to meet with Sun Yat-sen, and there are still his articles—in old newspapers, of course, under the title "My meetings with Sun Yat-sen." [6]

How were we brought up in those times? We had a terrible fear of becoming "bourgeois." It was terrible to be bourgeois, it was the most awful punishment one could suffer. Therefore, we were taught not to dress stylishly, one should not accumulate money, one could not do anything, in fact, except work hard and remain loyal. In general, we were taught modesty in everything. And God forbid that we wear the wrong clothes—garments that were provocative or challenging!

Among my possessions I had a Buddhist amulet. On the way to Moscow I caught a very severe chill. The doctor came, and on see-ing the amulet that I was wearing he was about to throw it out. But I seized it and hid it, and I therefore still have it preserved.

That was how I grew up—in an ultra-communist family, where I was taught that it was wrong to dress smartly, and that I must be practical and work as hard as possible. I finished school well. I learned Russian easily. Our primary school probably lasted around three years. We had a wonderful Russian teacher—Anna Petrovna Aleksich, a well-known specialist in teaching method, and everyone studied with her. Altogether we had very good teachers. The sister of Vladimir Ilyich [Lenin] used to come to the school, and we would warn his nephew, "Vitya, your auntie's come to see you."

It was a time of hunger, and we were all terribly hungry despite the fact that we received a Kremlin ration allocation. But that was only once a month—some caviar, a little meat and something else. But Communist Party members received the maximum—up to the value of 310 roubles. Well, they truly were really good communists. Nowadays, everyone says that the communists were this, that and the other, but I'm very grateful to those communists who brought me up and educated me. I'm not at all envious of people. I worked in the Ministry of Foreign Affairs and had splendid relations with everyone, and never envied anyone. Because we were taught that to envy people was nasty and disgraceful. This was the communist morality. And it was how I also tried to live.

In 1941, when war broke out, I was in Moscow. I had a Mongolian passport. I lived at that time very far from the centre, in the Stalinsky Region, at Kuntsevo, where the "Elektrosila" factory was. And by the time I went to our embassy on the Frunzenskaya Embankment, there was no longer anyone there. It was the month of July and bombing had already started. Only a guard was left on duty there and he told me, "Everyone's left already. Probably you're the only one remaining. There was just one other Mongolian here today. They've all left for Kuibyshev." In short, the entire diplomatic staff had been transferred. Then I went to the local visa office. There they told me, "You know, we're also being evacuated right now. You'll have to go to the Far East, because you won't get into Mongolia. You can't go to Kuibyshev either, because you don't have a visa." And since at that time we were all very law-abiding, and since the visa office had written a directive for me to go "To the Amur Region," I accordingly set off for the Far East.

When we arrived there, I immediately had to register with the militia. They were terribly scared: "In the Khabarovsk region there's not a single foreigner here apart from yourself," they said. "Why have you come here?" they asked. I told them, "But this is what they wrote, here..." But at that time nobody knew anything about Mongolia, and since I have such an oriental face, they thought all the time that maybe I was a spy—Japanese, or maybe someone else's spy. Well, they settled me near some of the camps in the Gulag. They told me I wasn't allowed to leave, and that I must come and report every month, until a "personal file" arrived for me. And the place where they sent me was very hard to reach— it meant a very long journey, to a small settlement called Chekunda where the militia station was; it could be reached in summer by boat along the River Bureya, but in winter you simply had to go on foot.

And the things I witnessed because of my Mongolian passport! Well, because I was a law-abiding person, I used to go all the time and report. And each time they asked me, "Where is your personal file?" But I had no idea what "personal file" they meant. Then at last it actually arrived from Moscow, because the visa office didn't know initially that I'd been dispatched to the Amur Region.

I lived there in the camp area for six years, and it was there in 1943 that I got to know Anastasiya Ivanovna Tsvetaeva, the sister of Marina the poet. At that time she was serving a sentence in the camps. She had been charged according to Article 54-10, I think, for "agitating against Soviet rule." All the same she was allowed to walk freely around the camp. She and I became great friends. We used to meet every day, and in summer and autumn we sat for long hours behind the school building, where nobody could find us.

During the Second World War few people were familiar with the writings of Marina Tsvetaeva. Anastasiya Ivanovna told me about their childhood and youth, how the two of them used to recite Marina's poetry in unison, what sort of people surrounded them at that time, how they went to stay in Koktebel at the house of Maksimilian Voloshin,[7] and how Marina got to know her husband Sergei Efron[8] there. She told me how Marina had perished in Elabuga in 1941, and about the disappearance of her son Georgii in the war. She told me she had found out everything from the letters of their friends. Anastasiya Ivanovna and I talked every day about Marina, we sorrowed together over her tragic fate and that of Sergei Efron, their daughter Alya and son Georgii (nicknamed "Mur"). Anastasiya Ivanovna remembered Marina's early verses and she wrote them down in a small notebook and gave them to me to keep. "After all, Marina's verses will be read by someone at some time!" she said.

Of herself, Anastasiya Ivanovna recounted that at one time she had been absorbed by the God-seeking movement when she stayed as a guest of Gorky in Italy. She also told me a lot about Boris Pasternak, with whom she had a correspondence. She was the kindest of people. She shared with me her piece of prisoners' black bread—during the war everyone experienced terrible problems with food and bread. In the summer we fed on goosefoot weed...

When Anastasiya Ivanovna was freed and she returned to Moscow, I immediately sent her the notebook containing Marina's verses, and she was very grateful. Then she and I used to meet in

Moscow. We talked a great deal, recalling our life in Izvestkovaya and Tyrma, and our friends who had been serving sentences in the camp: a former actress from the Maly Theatre called Urusova, the actor Gerken, Doctor Dieterichs, Etchin, who was the former secretary of Chicherin (The People's Commissar for Foreign Affairs), and many others. In Moscow, Anastasiya Ivanovna walked around in an old-fashioned coat she had found somewhere in her clothes chest. Because of that, when she and I were out walking together, people kept giving us awful looks. She was a very jolly person and always laughed at the fact that we both looked so strange—so out-of-date—apart from which I didn't look at all Russian. There were always young men and young girls at her home, although it was not clear what their interests were. When I came to see her, without paying any attention to the others present, Anastasiya Ivanovna would suddenly address a question to me: "Inochka, do you remember the name of the man who was the *operchek* in our camps?"—I answered that "I think it was Comrade Karelin," or some other name. And she said, "Ah, yes, yes!" And the young people looked very surprised and wondered who this "*operchek*" man was—in our time nobody knew what the word meant.

At one of our meetings in Moscow Anastasiya Ivanovna gave me a little aluminum cross, perhaps the work of some craftsman in the camps, and I have religiously preserved it ever since. I also preserved the letters she wrote after we parted company in the Far East, as well as her book of reminiscences, some issues of the journal *Moskva* from 1990 containing her novel *Amor*, and some articles she also gave me.

I eventually returned to Mongolia in 1947, having spent the whole of the war in the Far East. And when I arrived in Ulan-Bator, everyone again decided that I was a spy. I was summoned constantly by the KGB. One Russian general questioned me: "Where have you come from?"—"From the Far East," I answered.—"What for? Why were you living there? What were you doing there?" I told him, "I was sent there… I was working there."—"And how do we know that you were working there? The proper place for you is in prison." Those were his words. And I answered him: "Well, by all means. If you have such a law that allows you to put me in prison, then get on with it. I agree." Then the general shouted at me, "Get out of here!" In fact he yelled in such a terrifying manner that even his secretary could not stand it, and ran out of the room.

For a long time after that, and until Khrushchev gave his anti-Stalin speech [1956],[9] I was listed as a spy—now German, now Japanese… That's exactly what they said. We had there a city committee of the Party. I wasn't a Party member, of course, and the Secretary of the City Committee had said in front of everyone, "She's a spy, she's someone we have to be very careful with." This was openly reported back to me. I went to see him and banged my fist down on his desk. (After living in Russia for so long, I'd mastered this Russian habit!) The Secretary immediately became worried and asked, "What's the matter with you?" I asked him, "Why are you, as Secretary of the City Committee, saying that I am a spy? Where have you heard this from?" He of course denied having said anything of the sort, but I insisted and demanded a reply, since I had to find work for myself somewhere… But this sort of thing in fact went on for several years. Even when I worked in the Ministry of Foreign Affairs, all the time they kept listening in to my telephone. They thought I knew nothing about it. But all the time I kept hearing the click when they switched on at eight o'clock in the morning, and again when they switched off at night. But what could I say? Who could I speak to?

I was also well acquainted with Yury Nikolayevich Rerikh (Roerich), the Russian oriental scholar, who was the son of a remarkable artist. I had long been interested in the paintings of Nikolai Rerikh and especially liked the one called "Celestial Battle," which hangs in the Russian Museum in Saint Petersburg. Our own well-known scholar and author Damdinsuren corresponded with Yury Nikolayevich when he was still living in Kalimpong in India. Once the two of us wrote a joint letter to Yury Nikolayevich, mentioning his father and his remarkable works, and soon afterwards I received a letter with some small reproductions from his Himalayan period. Then Yury Nikolayevich came to Mongolia. This was in the summer of 1958, before a Congress of Mongolian scholars. I was immediately informed by telephone that Rerikh had come to Ulan-Bator and wanted to meet with me. On July 31, Yury Nikolayevich visited my modest home. He gave me a *Catalogue of the Exhibition of Works by Academician N. K. Rerikh*. At that time we lived in great poverty, we had one little room and in it there were almost only books. Yury Nikolayevich was accompanied by a Dr. Bira,[10] whom I didn't know well. Yury Nikolayevich said he was very glad to see me, he had got my letters and asked whether I had received his. I said "Yes, yes, thank you very much." But at that time you know how everything was. I was terribly afraid, and Rerikh had not come alone, but with Bira. Then Yury Nikolayevich asked, "Tell me, please, when was Professor Jamsran arrested?" O my God! I knew all this, and I remembered everything: it was in the year 1937, on August 4. But I was so afraid of this man Bira that I could not say anything and only answered vaguely, "Yes, I think it was in such and such a year..." Then Yury Nikolayevich asked, "And did you know Nikolai Nikolayevich Poppe?"[11] Of course I knew Poppe very well. He used to invite me to the theatre and the two of us used to walk together. But during the War he was a Nazi collaborator and he left Kalmykia together with the retreating Germans. He was an extremely pleasant man, despite the fact that he left the country. And as a scholar he was outstanding. But in answer to Rerikh's question I could not discuss Poppe, and I said only, "You know, I don't recall exactly." At that time it was a very frightening issue. Poppe was considered to be an enemy, so I said nothing about the theatre visits or any other details. Meanwhile, Nikolai Poppe always sent his greetings to me via Damdinsuren. When he lived in America, his letters at least got through, and he always wrote: "Pass my greetings on..." And of course I asked Damdinsuren to convey my greetings to him. But Yury Nikolayevich kept on asking me who had been arrested, where and when, but at that time, in 1958, I could tell him nothing, absolutely nothing. He was probably surprised that I said nothing and kept silent the whole time. But I did not know who this man Bira was, and at that time we all lived under the same God. But why bother talking about the subject?... In any case they still wrote all sorts of rubbish about me. If one could have seen my dossier, it would probably have been a very fat one.

Then, I met Rerikh again in 1960. It suddenly turned out that they were sending a delegation of Mongolian women to Copenhagen to attend some Congress. I was included entirely by chance. I had some artist friends—L. Gavaa and N. Tsultem, both of them now deceased. Tsultem died fairly recently. But then it was necessary to organize some women's exhibition, and Tsultem said of me that "She is suitable, because she knows how to set things up; she'll organize a good exhibition." And someone there in the Central Committee put my name down, and that was how I got accepted and approved. I was terribly surprised to be going to a Congress in Copenhagen, but also very glad. But not long before that some women had come to Mongolia from India. I knew a little English, and the visitors had asked me, "How many inhabitants are there in Ulan-Bator?" Well, at that time there were around 360,000, and that was what I said. But somebody immediately went and reported on me, claiming that I was betraying secret information to some foreign women. The visitors also asked whether I read any American writers, and I answered that, yes, I read Hemingway. And that was reported too: here's this woman who reads American writers, and she admitted it herself! And when the Indian delegation left, our women held a meeting, and the chairman told me, "You know, we're not going to send you after all. You passed on secret information to those Indian women." I protested to him, "Only see for yourself: it's written everywhere that in Moscow there are so many inhabitants, in the whole of Russia—so many, in London—so many, and in other cities too! It's not a secret." The answer was, "Well, we don't know. Nobody gave you authority to say how many residents there are in Ulan-Bator. And then, why are you reading this... Hemingway?" I told them that recently Mikoyan had been in America and had even met with him. Then I got really angry myself and said, "And now you're going to be sending these people, but I shan't be going anywhere." Then, however, they summoned me again and said, "You have to go. You're going to take an exhibition there." And I answered, "Okay, very well, very well." And I went off to prepare myself. But when I saw what this exhibition consisted of, I almost fainted! There was only a collection of some headscarves that had been sent by local women's organizations. Furthermore, they were so dirty and covered in stains, it was something terrible. And they couldn't be laundered clean. The times were like that. It was the year 1960. "Do you really not have anything else?" I asked. "No, no," came the answer, "but we do have a portrait of Choibalsan,[12] and then we have to hang up our coat of arms."—"Very well, okay," I said. So I took what was on offer.

But there were people who also constantly suspected me of espionage activities and kept following me around. A Japanese women's delegation came and talked and wanted to see what these Mongolians were like. They said, "Come on, let's sing a song."— "Very well," I agreed, "which song?"—"Haru Koro Karakora," they said. It was a very well-known song, and I knew it and sang it with them. Then, O Lord, what do you think happened?! "She really is a spy, she's singing a Japanese song!" Then there was another very well-known song, "Kojo No Tsuki." It described the moonlight falling on an old castle that was ruined when the Samurai went to war, but now it was spring, and so on. It was the sort of thing quite commonplace in Japanese poetry. There was absolutely nothing political about it. But then came the Americans, and on such occasions they usually sing an old Scottish song. I knew this one as well, and I sang along with them. Then I immediately became an American spy. And this was a song that people sang everywhere, absolutely everywhere! But there was no way of persuading anyone.

We returned via Moscow. Just at that time Sambu Jamsarangiin, President of the Presidium of the Great People's Khural of the Mongolian People's Republic was there, and a reception was organized for him in the Kremlin. Our women's delegation had also been invited. This was my first time in the Grand Kremlin Palace. There I also met Yury Nikolayevich Rerikh again. I explained to him that at our first meeting in Mongolia I had been unable to tell him anything because I was very afraid of Bira. Yury Nikolayevich was surprised: "Why were you afraid of him? He's my pupil," he said. And I told him. "We all live under the same God," I said. I don't know whether or not he understood me. Probably he did, because after that he and I went on to have a very good conversation. This all took place in spring, at the end of April, and in May Rerikh died.

He told me that a campaign was then being waged against Rinchen,[13] and they were collecting signatures, and all the Academicians were signing a letter attacking him. Rinchen is regarded as having been the first dissident in Mongolia. He corresponded with many scholars. Yury Nikolayevich said, "Right now they are collecting signatures against Rinchen, but I haven't signed, although they came and asked me..." At that time a *History of Mongolia* had just appeared, and some scholar, an Academician said, "Doctor Rinchen, the *History of Mongolia* has just come out." But Rinchen said nothing. "Have you read it?" the scholar persisted. Then Rinchen answered and said, "It's a load of shit!" and then he turned and left. The other Academician was terribly surprised. Well... and that was when the persecution began.

"You know," Rerikh added, "I thought that in Russia things would go well for me, but it turns out that... I'm depressed by the fact that when I walk into the Institute of Oriental Studies, I have to hang up a numbered token, and when I leave I have to hang up another token. This is killing me. It's terrible! I lived so well in Kalimpong, you could see the mountains from there. But here in Russia, I find life difficult. I thought that maybe in Mongolia it would be slightly better." I was about to tell him that we had the same thing, only worse, but I refrained. "I find life very difficult," he said. "And then, they've given me such a tiny apartment—my books won't fit into it. I brought all my books here, but they simply won't fit in."

Yury Nikolayevich and I spoke again in the Palace of Congresses about his life, how he was, what he was doing now, and what he was writing.

He was dressed in a very old-fashioned manner. He had on a *kazakin* [a knee-length coat with pleated skirt], or it may even have been a military-style khaki service jacket with brown boots. This astounded all of us. The first thing about him that struck people was his old-fashioned appearance. I liked Yury Nikolayevich very much, he was a splendid person and a remarkable scholar. Later on I read his books, about his trip to Tibet—*Along the Paths of Central Asia (Po tropam Sredinnoi Azii)*, and his *Selected Works (Izbrannye trudy)*. Apart from this, I had long been fond of the works of his father, the artist Nikolai Rerikh. I had seen them in Leningrad and at other exhibitions.

Lev Nikolayevich was also so well-disposed toward me because I knew and loved the verse of his father, the poet Nikolai Gumilev. I knew many of them by heart and probably I still remember them now. When he was in Paris in 1917, Nikolai Gumilev wrote a cycle of poems called *The Blue Star*. And I liked it when Lev Nikolayevich later called *me* his "Blue Star." But this was something so personal... Once he said to me, "Now, if you and I had got married just then, we would have had children. But now our families have come to an end—the family line of the Tsvetaevs, the Akhmatovs and the Gumilevs has ended. But if we had only had children..." But just then he was immediately arrested, and nothing came of this. So there's no need to talk about it. His wife, Natalya Viktorovna, once said, "He loved you very greatly, all his life. He is the sort of man who only loves one woman. Now I am going to leave you. You two have a talk, and I'm going." And so on that occasion we sat and talked. It was then that he talked about having children. But you know, it was also very hard for me to talk to him. So I left. In his last letters to me Lev Nikolayevich all the time kept asking whether I was happy in this life. He wrote, "I loved you sincerely..." Now his books are still left to me, written in the sort of brilliant Russian that only the son of Nikolai Gumilev and Anna Akhmatova could write.

I would like to visit the Aleksandro-Nevsky Lavra in Saint Petersburg, where the ashes of Lev Nikolayevich Gumilev are buried, and burn some incense. But unfortunately this is just as difficult for me as it is for a poor Muslim to make a pilgrimage to Mecca...

NAMSRAIJAV OCHIR:
LETTERS TO LEV GUMILEV
(1970-1991)

Translated by Christopher Barnes

1

Ulan-Bator, 24 March 1970

I was cheered by your letter, so much so that the Eternal Blue sky of Mongolia and the ancient Bogd Uul mountains seem to rejoice together with me at my happiness.

All these years I have remembered you and our meeting long ago, and your interesting article only helped me to find you.

If you can send me your book, I shall be eternally glad and grateful to you, my friend.

I am getting ready to go to Moscow with our delegation, where I shall be for just four days. Unlike you, who is a scholar, I am a functionary, almost the fourteenth grade!

But I think and permit myself to hope that you will not disdain your poor Mongolian functionary and will occasionally write to her?

Are you coming to see us? Then you could spend some time in the Gobi, maybe, at Gurvan Saikhan,[14] and also visit Kara-Korum.[15] Manai Gov'[16] (the Gobi) is splendid in the summer with the endless blue of the horizon, with its mirages, the smell of wormwood, and the vultures soaring high... Do come to Mongolia!

Ever your *Namsraijav*

Ulan-Bator, 14 September 1970

Arslan min',[17]

How are you? When did you get back to Leningrad? I have been away for the entire summer and therefore did not write to you.

Over this period we have had the Second Congress of Mongolists. There were many people from other countries. Unfortunately, I cannot describe anything in detail about the Congress since I was not in Ulan-Bator. But after it was over I did see comrades Lattimore,[18] Gombojav and others. I asked comrade Gombojav about Nikolai Nikolayevich P[oppe]. He said he had returned from Bonn to the USA.

It's a great pity that you were not able to be at this Congress. When I enquired, our Academy answered that they sent only the number of invitees to various countries, but without indicating any names. But in 1971 we would have been able to send you a private invitation, with the idea that you could come to see us at a time convenient to yourself. We will all be glad to have you visit us.

The materials of the Congress will be published in 1971, so it will be possible to acquaint oneself with all the papers and reports. Incidentally, from Australia came a Dr. Igor de Rachewiltz, who has tried with the help of a computer to Latinize the words of the Mongolian text of the "Secret Legend." I remember that last year I read his article about this experiment.

How did the historians' forum go in Moscow?

Will your book soon appear?[19] We are awaiting it impatiently in Mongolia.

Please write, *Arslan min'* , if you can find the time, and I will be very glad and grateful to you.

Your *Namsraijav*

3

Ulan-Bator, 21 October 1970

Arslan min',

Your letter made me so glad, since there were no letters from you all summer, because I did not write to you either. I rejoice along with you that your book has appeared. Will it reach us here, and when? One can only guess.

I'll definitely send you an invitation. As soon as you arrive, we shall go and see Tonyukuk,[20] which is not far from Nalaikh,[21] and we'll put together an interesting programme for your stay in our country.

In response to your request I am sending some photographs which were ready to hand. I don't have a single "real" photograph because my face is not photogenic, with prominent cheekbones, and I look even more ugly and broad in the face. They were sent to me recently by some Bulgarian friends.

Comrade Maidar D.[22] is always asking about you, he wants to be introduced to you, since he knows you already from your works. He said that in late October or early November he will be in Moscow and may also pay a call to Leningrad in order to see you. Write, please, and say whether one or two meetings and a chat with him will not be too burdensome for you. He is the Deputy Chairman of the Council of Minister of the MPR and is a splendid (in the sense of "good") person.

I too would very much like to see you. In mid-November I will be in Moscow, en route to Berlin. But probably by this time you will already have returned to Leningrad.

Please send me your photograph.

Your *Namsraijav* (Mongolian functionary, fourteenth class)

4

2 November 1970

My dear love, [in English in the original]

After my "invasion" of your comfortable home, I have returned safely to my native city.

How are you feeling, and how did the discussion of your book go?

Doctor Rinchen was glad to learn of my meeting with you and said that you are a remarkable scholar. On the street I met Sandag, who asked about your book, since he has already heard about it. Our map of monasteries has not yet appeared. I have seen only the first proof copies. As soon as it appears, I will immediately send it to you.

How is your dear Natalya Viktorovna? I wanted to send her a postcard with a picture of a yak, but could not find one. As soon as I find one, I'll send it without delay...

We are having fine weather with frosts of up to minus 25 degrees, but we don't feel the cold at all, since there is a lot of sun.

Have you received my letter and the photo? Please write and tell me. Surely it has not got lost in the labyrinth of postal section *trois*. [in French in the original]

Wishing you great success, your *mongol femme* [*in French in the original*], with the permission of our Dear Mother![23] But for her, we'd have hardly had a chance to meet in Moscow.

I kiss and embrace Natalya Viktorovna and yourself.

Your *I. Ochir*

5

Ulan-Bator12 October 1974

Dear Lev Nikolayevich,

Forgive me for the long silence. I received your book *Khunny v Kitae* (*The Huns in China*) and have read it with immense interest. This last summer Owen Lattimore was here, he said of you that you write very romantically!

At last I am sending you a personal or, rather, private invitation.

We can start the registration process immediately, but you can come in spring or summer of 1975, as it suits you. Write and tell me, please, how they, i.e. the militia, responded to this invitation, whether they will register it. Maybe it will be necessary to forward various other "papers."

I recently returned from Sofia, where I was briefly on business. It was very warm, and the roses are still in blossom. I would have liked to go to Leningrad to see Natalya Viktorovna and yourself, but my sense of duty did not allow me! I had to get back in time to work, and so on and so forth.

Please, write. Many thanks for the book and for your letters.

Hoping to see you here and show you our country.

I kiss you.

Your *I. Ochir*

6

25 May 1976

Dear Lev Nikolayevich,

I received your postcard a long time ago, in which you wrote that you will not be able to come and visit us. I would like to send you and Natalya Viktorovna another invitation. Maybe your old Mother will permit the two of you to come and see us. Write and tell me what you think about this and what your plans are for the summer and autumn. How is your health and that of Natalya Viktorovna? It is possible to get here by train, you don't have to fly, if you find the flight difficult.

I heard that your book on Buryat iconography has appeared. It has not been on sale here.

In the fall of last year, when I stopped over in Moscow en route from Sofia, I met several times with Anastasiya Ivanovna Tsvetaeva, who used to call you by the affectionate diminutive Lyovushka. It was interesting to plunge oneself into the world of the old Russian intelligentsia, to visit those cramped Moscow apartments with their old books, and photographs from the nineteenth century. We walked around Moscow together, talked about Marina Tsvetaeva, and visited some common acquaintances.

It's a great pity that the years are going by and we see very little of each other. But we should have a talk about many things. Please write.

In the hope that we can meet soon,

Your *I. Ochir*
In the journal *Priroda* I read a review of *The Huns in China*

7

Ulan-Bator, 28 July 1979

Dear Lev Nikolayevich,

How are you feeling? How is Natalya Viktorovna?

I recently returned home,[24] and I am not going to go anywhere any more. I am enjoying the clean air, sunshine, and peace.

There I was struck by the architecture of the Winter and Summer Palaces, the temples of the Yuan dynasty, the numerous parks, and many other things. The climate is a difficult one for us: in summer there is moist heat, in spring there are winds that raise clouds of loss, the winter is not very pleasant, there is the heavy air of a city badly provided with services and utilities, crowds of people, etc. But it was still interesting to see another country and its people, and to travel around the country a little.

I am very glad that I can write letters to you—from there I could not write to you, unfortunately. Three years have gone by since I had any letters from you. Please write to me, I would be very, very glad. I am proud of the fact that I have your books: *The Ancient Turki* [*Drevnie tyurki*], *The Huns in China*, *The Quest for the Imaginary Kingdom*, and several articles.

What are you working on just now? Where are you thinking of spending the summer?

Recently at the Buddhist Forum in Ulan-Bator there was the fourteenth Dalai Lama. Tenzin Gyatso. I saw him every morning when he was processing up Gandan [25] with his entourage.

We are having a rainy summer here now, but, as always, there is plenty of sun and everything immediately dries out.

Over the short time I was away from Ulan-Bator much has changed. A lot of homes have been built, museum buildings, and other public institutions.

Dear Lev Nikolayevich, I hope you are enjoying good health, strength of spirit, and that you still remember your distant friend.

I kiss and embrace you tenderly,

Your *Namsraijav*
Kind regards to Natalya Viktorovna.

Ulan-Bator, 27 March 1989

Dear Lev Nikolayevich,

I don't know whether you received my greetings for the New Year of 1989, but in this year of the Yellow Snake I wish you and Natalya Viktorovna health, joy, and success in all your doings.

There is little time left (I have now reached the biblical age!) and I would like to see you again. Ever since 1937 to this day I love and respect you as my only close friend. Fate has not been kind to us, and I often think of those years, senseless in their cruelty, through which we have had to live.

Please do not forget me amid all your important daily affairs.

In our press they recently published an interview with you by the correspondent of the paper *Unen* (*Pravda*). It was very reassuring to hear about you specifically in our own paper. Many articles of various sorts also appear about Rinchen. All these are signs of perestroika going on in our country.

I suppose that you are very busy with the centenary of the birth of your mother Anna Andreyevna Akhmatova.

Wishing you and Natalya Viktorovna success.

Your *Namsraijav*, who embraces and kisses you

21 October 1991

Dear Lev Nikolayevich,

On the 14th of October of this year I received your splendid three books, about which I had heard so much, and one of them, *The Geography of Ethnos in the Historical Period,* they have also promised to send from Irkutsk. Many thanks for your attention and for the inscriptions which gladden me and lend me wings!

How are you feeling? A few days ago on our TV they showed you and Natalya Viktorovna, when one of our people (probably a journalist) offered you some *khadak,* a cup of milk, or *airag.* I was very glad to see you and Natalya Viktorovna, almost as if I had been with you in Leningrad.

I have returned from Beijing, where I spent about two weeks. In Beijing they are enjoying an opulent autumn: the whole city is full of yellow chrysanthemums and roses. On the streets are the spicy smell of greenery, an abundance of fruit, and sea fish.

I visited the Temple of Heaven, the Buddhist temple of Yonghegong, where I set up some lighted sticks of "diamond incense" for your and Natalya Viktorovna's health in front of the most hallowed spot in the temple. I was also in the Summer Palace of the Empress Tzu-hsi, and I walked across the marble bridge and stood by the marble ark.

I visited the Historical Museum where we were forbidden to go eleven years ago at the end of the "Cultural Revolution." The museum building is splendid. The ancient period of China is fairly well represented, and there are many objects of the material culture of those times. The Tang period is there, there is nothing on the Sun, it is rather brief on the Yuan, with slightly more on the Ming and Tsin. For some reason I expected more. What has been found in Siam, in the ancient capital of the Thai Empire, can only be seen in copies. Be that as it may, at least I did have a chance to visit this museum. I was several times on Tiananmen Square, where there were some stormy events some three years ago. Everything is as it was eleven years ago. There is a portrait of Mao and a new one of Sun Yat-sen.

The parks of Beijing are delightful. There are cypresses, ginkgo biloba with their fan-like leaves, a lot of flowers and relative peace and quiet, since in the streets there are a lot of people and you quickly get tired. I walked around in old Beijing, with its tiny narrow lanes and cramped courtyards. There is no space or horizon in sight. How people live in such confined spaces!

But perestroika has been a success. The city of a billion has been fed, clothed and shod. There are loads of produce and goods, and the prices are fairly normal. Nowhere did I see a line-up, but everyone is busy buying something. There are many little restaurants with superb Chinese cuisine.

I once even visited the Catholic Cathedral, erected by the Jesuit Father Adam Schall in 1650. A nice Chinese woman called Sister Bernadette showed us the cathedral and told us that at the present time there are forty thousand Catholics in Beijing, and six other Catholic churches are open. Overall, I was pleased with my trip.

Back home we are well into the autumn. Snow fell a long time ago, and has not melted in the mountains. But the sun is shining, and the temperature is minus seven degrees Centigrade at night, and plus seven degrees during daytime.

My thanks to Natalya Viktorovna for sending on the books. What a lot of labour it probably cost her to forward them. May God preserve you.

I kiss and embrace you.

Your *Namsraijav*

P.S. Please write postcards, at least to give me that joy. In China I kept thinking all the time: why in the years of our youth were we not allowed to visit China and other countries together?... We really did live behind an iron curtain, the devil knows!

10

Ulan-Bator, 16 December 1991

My dear, kind Lev Nikolayevich!

I have received your postcard. The tantric rituals will help us, and you and I will live long! And when you wrote me, you felt unwell because of the unfavourable days at the end of November and beginning of December. But now everything will be well. I will come to collect you and Natalya Viktorovna, and we shall steadily make our way to Ulan-Bator, we will travel around the various *aimags*, we'll breathe in the smells of wormwood on the steppes, we shall admire the sunrise and sunset in the Gobi, and the mirages, and this will strengthen your health, and you will feel extraordinarily cheerful and strong.

When many years have passed, and when the time comes, you and I will cross over the stony moss-covered little bridge in the radiance of the first morning rays and we shall see the house with the Venetian window and the curling grapevines. Here you will work on your favourite project, and, if you allow, I together with Natalya Viktorovna will preserve your peace, and nobody will ever part us, and we will be young again. That's how it will be according to Mikhail Bulgakov. [26]

And right now, every day at sunrise, I recite the ritual prayers of Tarni (Tantra) for your health. They are very powerful, these rituals, and everything will be well—just you see!

We are all enjoying reading your books. What superb language! How much material there is collected there and how interesting, and how unusually it is presented! Thank you for your invaluable works. May the Tantra preserve your health and strength!

Thank you for your love, which we have maintained through years of disaster and the impossibility of meeting. At that time Moscow, not to mention Petersburg, was a Mecca for us. Only a few chosen ones could visit it just then. For me the road there was closed. What a pity… But I am grateful to fate that we were able to meet twice over all this period (since 1937) and that we can now at least maintain a correspondence.

I embrace you, my dearly beloved.

Your *Namsraijav*

FOOTNOTES TO NAMSRAIJAV OCHIR

[1] Lev Nikolayevich Gumilev (1912-92)—distinguished Soviet Russian orientalist. He was the son of distinguished poets Anna Akhmatova and Nikolai Gumilev. By 1921, his mother's aesthetic non-conformism had led to her marginalization from Soviet poetry, a marginalization that blighted their son Lev's personal and professional life and caused his internment for several years under Stalin from 1937 to the 1950s. See also in "Notes to Mongolian Études." On Akhmatova and Nikolai Gumilev see also in "Notes to Mongolian Études."

[2] Anastasiya Ivanovna Tsvetaeva (1894-1993)—writer, memoirist and younger sister of the celebrated poet Marina Ivanovna Tsvetaeva (1892-1941)—celebrated Russian modernist poet, followed her husband into exile in 1919, going first to Berlin, Czechoslovakia and later to Paris; returned to Russia in 1939, where her husband and daughter Ariadna were arrested for alleged espionage; she failed to regain a professional foothold, and though evacuated along with other members of the Moscow literary community, she committed suicide in 1914.

[3] Yury Nikolayevich Rerikh (Roerich) (1902-60)—Russian orientalist, linguist and explorer; son of Nikolai (Nicholas) Roerich (1874-1947), celebrated artist, writer, philosopher.

[4] Nina Petrovna Tupoleva—sister-in-law of Andrei Nikolayevich Tupolev (1888-1972), the celebrated Soviet aircraft designer, who was arrested in 1937 on false charges of conspiracy and released

only in 1944 to continue his work. When he was interned, other close relatives shared his fate.

5 Kunstkamera—Russia's first museum, founded in 1721 by Peter the Great, initially famed as a collection of human and natural curiosities.

6 Sun Yat-sen (1866-1925)—Chinese revolutionary and first president of the Republic of China.

7 Maksimilian Aleksandrovich Voloshin (1877-1932)—Russian symbolist poet and painter who regularly played host to friends from the artistic intelligentsia at his house in Koktebel (later Planersoye) in the Crimea.

8 Sergei Yakovlevich Efron (1893-1941)—husband of Marina Tsvetaeva; joined the White Army and emigrated to Berlin after the Bolshevik revolution. After reunification with his family, nostalgia for his homeland drove him to collaborate in NKVD conspiratorial work; he fled back to Moscow in 1937 and was later rejoined there by Marina; he was arrested in 1939 and executed 1941.

9 Khrushchev's speech at the Twentieth Party Congress (1956) was a first official revelation of some of Stalin's major crimes and marked the beginning of a radical de-Stalinization and the reinforcement of an amnesty for those wrongly arrested and imprisoned.

10 Shagdaryn Bira (born 1927) Academician of the Mongolian Academy of Sciences. In 1957 he was a graduate student of Yury

Rerikh at the Soviet Academy of Sciences' Institute of Oriental Studies.

[11] Nikolai Nikolayevich Poppe (1897-1991)—Soviet scholar, author of numerous research publications on the Mongolian and Buryat languages. In 1943 he emigrated to Germany, then moved to the USA in 1949.

[12] Khorloogiin Choibalsan (1895-1952)—communist leader of the Mongolian People's Republic.

[13] Rinchen Byambyn (1905-77)—Mongolian writer and scholar, author of academic and belletristic books on the past history of the Mongolians. He was the husband of Namsraijav Ochir's elder sister.

[14] Gurvan Saikhan—the "Three Beauties," a mountain range in southern Mongolia.

[15] Kara-Korum (*Khara Khorin* in Mongolian)—the ancient capital of Mongolia, on its ruins the first lamasery of Erdenu Zuu was built.

[16] *Manai Gov'* (Mongolian)—our Gobi.

[17] *Arslan min'* (Mongolian)—my Lev (or lion).

[18] Owen Lattimore (1900-89)—American sinologist and explorer of Central Asia; Gombojav—American scholar and Mongolist; re N. N. Poppe, see above note 12.

[19] Lev Gumilev's *The Quest for the Imaginary Kingdom.*

[20] A complex of monuments from the late eighth century, including a monumental column with inscriptions. Tonyukuk was an adviser to the Turkic kogan.

[21] Nalaikh Soum—a major and spectacular mineral outcrop of granitic and other rocks.

[22] Maidar Damginjavyn—Mongolian scholar, Doctor of Historical Sciences, author of the books *Monuments of Mongolia's History and Culture (Pamyatniki istorii i kul'tury Mongolii)* and *Many-faced Mongolia. Ethnographical essays (Raznolikaya Mongoliya. Etnograficheskie ocherki).*

[23] Moscow, or the Soviet state.

[24] For some years Namsraijav Ochir had worked in China in the Mongolian Embassy.

[25] Gandan—the hill on which the Buddhist monastery of Gandantegchinlen stands.

[26] Mikhail Bulgakov (1891-1940)—the second paragraph of the letter is Namsraijav's fanciful vision of Lev Gumilev's future based on the afterlife of the hero of Mikhail Bulgakov's novel *The Master and Margarita.*

NOTES TO MONGOLIAN ÉTUDES

Anna Andreyevna Akhmatova (Gorenko) (1889-1966)—an outstanding Russian modernist poet, one of the most acclaimed writers in recent Russian literature. Like many of her family, she suffered under the Soviet regime. She was born into a Russian-Ukrainian family, but was proud to have some noble Mongolian roots. She was the mother of Lev Gumilev and the wife of Nikolai Gumilev.

Aleksandr Sergeyevich Pushkin (1799-1837)—Russian poet, an admirer of the English poet Lord Byron and one of the founders of modern Russian literature·. Born into the Russian nobility in Moscow, Pushkin wrote his first poems in French. One of his ancestors was a black Ethiopian nobleman, who was brought to Russia by Peter the Great. Notoriously touchy about his honour, Pushkin fought a total of twenty-nine duels, and was fatally wounded by d'Anthès, a French military officer who attempted to seduce the poet's wife. Pushkin's early death at the age of thirty-seven is regarded as a major catastrophe for Russian literature.

Amedeo Clemente Modigliani (1884-1920)—Italian painter and sculptor who worked mainly in France. He was primarily a figurative artist, known for paintings and sculptures in a modern style, which were characterized by mask-like faces and elongation of form. The original beautiful appearance of Anna Akhmatova, who was a friend of the artist in Paris in 1910-11, influenced him as a model for all his subsequent paintings.

Charles-Édouard Jeanneret, known as **Le Corbusier** (1887-1965)—architect, designer, urbanist, and writer, famous as one of the pioneers of what is now called modern architecture. He was born in Switzerland and became a French citizen in 1930. His career spanned five decades, and his buildings were erected throughout Europe, India and America.

Gerel Ochir (born 1941)—daughter of Namsraijav, professor, director of the Geoscience Center at the Mongolian University of Science and Technology. She graduated from the Charles University, Prague, in geology, and received a Ph.D in petrology, and a Doctor of Sciences degree in geochemistry from the scientific institutes of the Russian Academy of Sciences. She was head of the Department of Geology (1968-2008); she led a number of international projects, including the Canadian International Development Agency (CIDA) project on "Education for Environmental Transition: Mining in Mongolia" (2004-10). She is also an Honorary Scientist of Mongolia, leader and member of many professional organizations.

Genghis Khan (1162-1227)—Mongolian warlord who consolidated nomadic tribes into a unified Mongolia, creating the basis for one of the greatest continental empires of all time. He proclaimed himself in 1206 as the Universal Ruler, and in less than ten years conquered most of the Euro-Asian world. He was infamous for slaughtering the entire populations of conquered lands, but admired for his military brilliance and learning ability.

Golden Horde—the group of settled, Turkicized Mongols who ruled over Russia, Ukraine, Kazakhstan, Moldova and the Caucasus from the 1240s until 1502. It was established by Batu Khan, a grandson of Genghis Khan.

Khulan Tserenjav—granddaughter of Namsraijav, born in 1968. She graduated from the Faculty of Philosophy of Moscow State University; she also holds a Master's degree in International Relations from the New South Wales University of Australia. Since 1997 she worked in the mining industry in Mongolia, and currently works in the Rio Tinto Exploration office in Mongolia.

L'Architecture d'Aujourd'hui—the oldest French architecture magazine. It was created during the economic crisis, in November 1930. From its very first issue, *L'Architecture d'Aujourd'hui* promoted the avant-garde and various movements and personalities. Le Corbusier was an active supporter of the magazine. At this time, it was the only French architecture magazine known worldwide. Starting from the 1950s, *L'Architecture d'Aujourd'hui* was for a long time almost the only source of information on international contemporary architecture available to Soviet architects.

Lev Nikolayevich Gumilev (1912-92)— the Russian historian, ethnologist and anthropologist. His unorthodox ideas on the birth and death of ethnic groups (*ethnoi*) have given rise to the political and cultural movement known as "Neo-Eurasianism."

Ludwig Mies van der Rohe (1886-1969)—German-American architect. Along with Walter Gropius, Le Corbusier and Oscar Niemeyer, he is widely regarded as one of the pioneering masters of modern architecture. He created an influential international architectural style, stated with extreme clarity and simplicity and using modern materials such as industrial steel and plate glass. He called his buildings "skin and bones" architecture. He is often associated with the aphorisms "less is more" and "God is in the details."

Mongolia—country located in East and Central Asia and bordered by Russia, China, and Kazakhstan. The area of what is now Mongolia has been ruled by various nomadic empires. In the sixteenth century, Mongolia came under the influence of Tibetan Buddhism. The country was under strong Soviet Russian influence from 1924. In 1989, Mongolia became an independent Democratic Republic.

Namsraijav Ochir (1915-2004)—the activist in the International Women's Movement. She was born in Mongolia, but lived in Soviet Union for twenty years during WWII and the Stalinist repressions. The life of Namsraijav Ochir was closely connected with many outstanding figures in Russian culture and politics. After WWII she lived in Ulan-Bator working for the Ministry of Foreign Affairs. In 1970, during construction of the Soviet Embassy in Ulan-Bator, she was a Mongolian government supervisor.

Nikolai Stepanovich Gumilev (1886-1921)—influential Russian poet, who founded the modernist Acmeist movement in poetry. He was executed by the Bolsheviks. He was the husband of Anna Akhmatova and the father of the ethnologist Lev Gumilev.

Nikolai Mikhailovich Karamzin (1766-1826)—Russian writer, poet, critic and historian. He is best remembered for his *History of the Russian State*, a twelve-volume national history.

Phags-pa Lama (1235-80)—Tibetan scholar and monk who set up a Buddhist theocracy in Tibet. After the Mongols had established suzerainty over his country, Phags-pa visited Mongolia in 1247 to help promote the implantation of Buddhism. Phags-pa had great influence with Kublai Khan, ruler of the Yuan dynasty (1206–1368) of China. Phags-pa was the inventor of an alphabet for the Mongol language. Its widespread use was limited to about a hundred years during the Yuan dynasty, and it fell out of use with the advent of the Ming dynasty.

Semyon Nikolaevich Tshetinin (1912-75)—Soviet diplomat and ambassador in Mongolia 1968-75.

Timur (1336-1405), historically known as **Tamerlane**—Turkic ruler who conquered West, South and Central Asia and founded the Timurid dynasty. Timur envisioned the restoration of the Mongol Empire of Genghis Khan. Unlike his predecessors, Timur was a devout Muslim and referred to himself as "The Sword of Islam." His military campaigns caused the deaths of seventeen million people, amounting to about five percent of the world population.

ACKNOWLEDGEMENTS

I had the idea some time ago to write a book about my business trip to Soviet Mongolia. I wanted to write about a woman who had worked with me as the representative of the Mongolian Government. I wanted also to touch on her friendship with the remarkable Russian scientist/orientalist, Lev Gumilev. Recently, after I'd found a way to make contact, that woman's daughter sent me her mother's memoirs. I'd like to thank my new Mongolian friend Gerel Ochir, for her participation in this project and for being the first to read the manuscript.

The Editor-in-Chief of Exile Editions, Barry Callaghan, has a unique knowledge of Russian culture and literature. He has visited Russia several times. I'd like to say a huge thank you to him for his work. I am especially grateful for his skilful and passionate commitment to our translation of the poems of Anna Akhmatova. A special thank you to Christopher Barnes, Professor of Slavic Languages and Literatures of Toronto University, for his vibrant work as the translator of Namsraijav Ochir's dramatic memoires To publisher Michael Callaghan, thank you for publishing this book, and for your devotion to book design that always brings out the best in the material you have to work with

Vladimir Azarov is an architect and poet,
formerly from Moscow, who lives in Toronto.
His books include *Seven Lives: Short Stories in Verse,*
Territories, Night Out, Dinner With Catherine the Great,
Strong Words (a bilingual edition with Barry Callaghan),
Of Life and Other Small Sacrifices, Imitation,
The Kiss from Mary Pickford: Cinematic Poems,
Voices in Dialogue: Dramatic Poems.